THE A TO Z OF
The Curiosity Approach®

BY LYNDSEY HELLYN & STEPHANIE BENNETT

**Copyright © 2021 The Curiosity Approach®.
All rights reserved.**

First published in 2017.

This edition published 2021 by The Curiosity Approach® ~ www.thecuriosityapproach.com
ISBN 978-1-9998762-2-7

Printed in Great Britain

Cover design by Stephanie Breen
Cover image ID 54911258 © Lisaalisaill | Dreamstime

Book design by Design Dejour ~ www.design-dejour.co.uk

No part of this book can be reproduced in any form or by written, electronic or mechanical means, including photocopying, recording, or by any information retrieval system without written permission in writing by the author.

Photography courtesy of The Nest Nursery, The Nest Nursery Wood End, The Nest Nursery Copper Beech, The Nest Nursery Lime Tree, Love 2 Learn Nursery and Kidaroo Childcare.

Photographers ~ Laura Wragg and Radomir Kos

Although every precaution has been taken in the preparation of this book, the publisher and author assume no responsibility for errors or omissions. Neither is any liability assumed for damages resulting from the use of information contained herein.

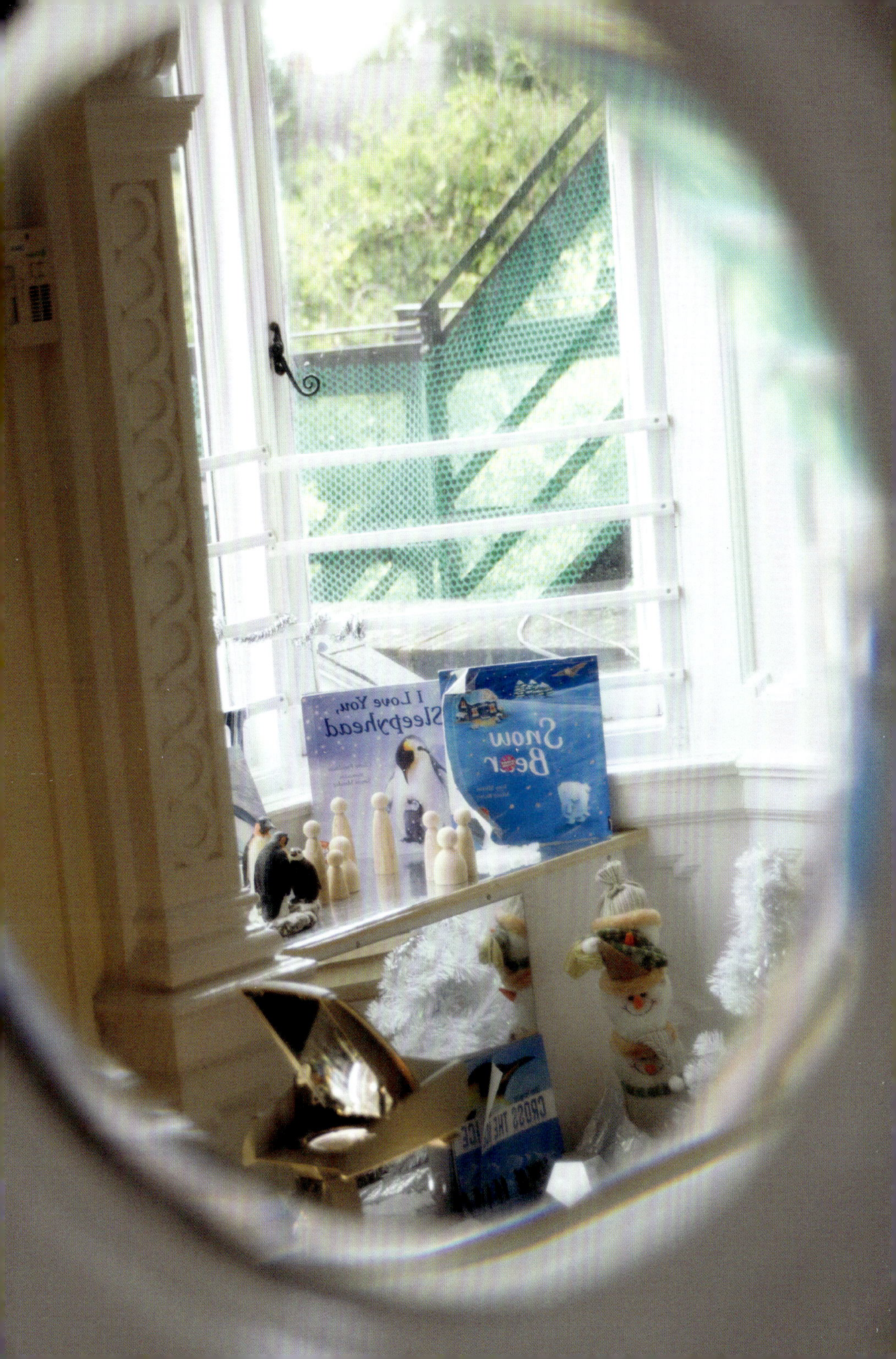
I Love You, Sleepyhead
Snow Bear

Welcome!

...TO THE A TO Z OF THE CURIOSITY APPROACH®

The Curiosity Approach® is more than just beautiful play spaces. It's a modern day approach to Early Years taking parts from Reggio, Steiner, Te Whāriki and a sprinkle of Montessori.

It's a beautiful recipe book of wonderful ingredients, carefully mixed together with experience, passion and a love of early childhood.

It's baked together in a mindful oven of loveliness that needs thoughtful practitioners and professionals to be mentally present, thankful and forever curious about their career with little children.

This is modern day approach that fits perfectly into current changing technological times. Bringing curiosity, awe and wonder into early childhood and creating the 'thinkers and doers' of the future.

Over time we have learned that by getting the learning environment right you are taking massive action in embedding and protecting the innate skills of the child; curiosity, awe and wonder. The learning environment should be your 'buddy', your 'best friend' who supports you in nurturing these miracles we are presented with each day. So treat 'her' well and look after her carefully for together you will create environments that are worthy of children's immense capabilities.

Our A-Z guide will give you endless gateways, ideas and tools to bring The Curiosity Approach® to your setting.

Lyndsey Hellyn and Stephanie Bennett are the founders of The Curiosity Approach®. Together they have over 50 years teaching and leadership experience in early childhood. They are the directors of four settings across the West Midlands in the UK.

Lyndsey began her career as a primary school teacher in Birmingham, leading a range of early years departments from neighbourhood nurseries to children's centres. In 2009 she became the proud owner of her first private setting. Using her previous knowledge of child development and her visits to Reggio Emilia, Italy, Lyndsey has created environments where staff are empowered, supported and inspired to work to the highest standard.

Stephanie Bennett qualified in childcare over 30 years ago and has an Early Years degree with 'Early Years Professional Status'. She is the passionate and inspirational owner of two incredible nurseries in Leicestershire. She is a huge advocate of young children's learning and is dedicated to raising standards in early years provision by motivating practitioners to provide the most wondrous opportunities for children.

Lyndsey and Stephanie aim to take you on a journey, helping you to revamp and develop your educational play space into a beautiful, purposeful and enabling environment, along with helping you to understand why you are doing it! This step-by-step guide will give you the tools and knowledge to transform your setting. Whether you are a newly qualified practitioner, educator, childminder or Early Years teacher, this book is for you.

Enjoy!

STEPHANIE BENNETT & LYNDSEY HELLYN

www.thecuriosityapproach.com

CHILDREN ARE NATURALLY *curious!*

We need to encourage and inspire that curiosity and develop their creativity... but that takes work from you.

Children of today need different skills. In the digital age, they need to be able to IMAGINE the future... then build it!

Children are natural learners, and in the words of Whitney Houston:

> **CHILDREN ARE OUR FUTURE**
> **TEACH THEM WELL AND LET THEM LEAD THE WAY**
> **SHOW THEM ALL THE BEAUTY THEY POSSESS INSIDE**
> **GIVE THEM A SENSE OF PRIDE TO MAKE IT EASIER.**
>
> *Whitney Houston*

Instead of restricting our children, we encourage them to explore, to create, to be curious. We show you how throughout this book.

Our mission is to inspire a generation of thinkers and doers - to achieve that; we need to inspire you!

What our community are saying...

Amy Jane Bayliss · 4 w

I simply wouldn't be in Early Years anymore if it wasn't for The Curiosity Approach. Its changed me as a practitioner and changed my personal life too all for the greater good. My little ones are thriving everyday through the power of Curiosity and Play! Its more than an Accreditation its joining a family of like minded people putting Early Years at the centre of the Heart. Once you start to learn more about The Curiosity Approach you find your WHY and find that curious person within yourself 🌟 The journey is incredible and I want to shout this out to the whole 🌍 x

Karean Carr · 4 w

In a nut shell I am passionate and motivated everyday. The Curiosity Approach has sparked a new lease of life inside of me as I felt lost and so Un - inspired before. Children think and use their imaginations more and you can see and feel that Awe and wonder

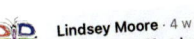

Lindsey Moore · 4 w

Magical - Life changing approach, Changed the way I think about my learning environment, changed the way my staff think about their working ethic- As a team we became a reflective team, always asking who, why and what for.
Provision - Offered more open ended resources, children play more deeply with resources. Seen a positive change in the children's attention to play.
Highly recommend the approach to everyone we come across and it's something I feel more forest schools should embed.
The CA journey fits perfectly for the FS ethos

Becki Agar

The curiosity approach has enabled me to create the space and given me the tools to inspire children to just be their unique selves. The little ones are excited to come in and explore, they engage with the environment and without realising it their curiosities are leading them to flourish and learn through the most imaginative, creative play. Losing themselves in 'magical' experiences that I feel immensely proud when I see them meet that next step and they get excited about their own achievements. The children are creators of their own stories, their imaginations and creations are extended through a text rich environment surrounded by wonder and awe. Authentic and open-ended resources give them endless opportunities to act out, create, experiment, develop conversation and give them learning opportunities naturally without them being driven. The children lead every step of the way, developing at their own pace whilst being encouraged to succeed and unfold naturally, following the child and their interests is so refreshing and uplifting. It is exciting to see what journey they will take me on next, "their journey is my journey". The curiosity approach has been an exciting experience that I will cherish and will continue to keep developing and applying.

· Like · Reply · 4w

www.thecuriosityapproach.com

A

AUTHENTIC RESOURCES

At The Curiosity Approach®, we absolutely love authentic resources, recycled materials and loose parts.

We spend endless hours searching car boots for eclectic resources for children to handle investigate and explore. As part of The Curiosity Approach®, we aim to ensure that environments and children's play spaces offer a calm and tranquil place to become engaged in deep levels of sustained thinking.

A Curiosity Approach educational setting would be adorned with authentic resources, wooden items, baskets and a natural tranquil feel throughout.

A car boot, charity or op shop is an ideal place to find authentic resources and wooden natural treasures. Wooden items are incredibly special and we are extremely lucky to be able to handle, explore and investigate infinitely variable and immensely beautiful wood ranging from wicker baskets to native carvings or exquisite hardwoods.

These durable authentic resources offer children the opportunity to experience nature first hand and become connected to our natural world through play. Just as importantly, by recycling and reusing authentic resources we are ensuring that we do our small bit for the environment and prevent these beautiful items going into landfill before their time.

Swap from the plastic...

Plastic tea sets up and down the country last for years – they get dropped and thrown, used in the water play area or in the outside sand pit. They get coloured or scribbled on, sometimes scratched and occasionally chewed. They get flung across the room or dumped without care or regard. Children subconsciously and consciously know this, they think it's ok to treat these resources any way they like because these items are virtually indestructible. So, is this a good thing?

There are therefore no consequences to children's actions – it really doesn't matter if a tea cup gets catapulted across the home corner, or a saucer literally becomes a flying missile from one side of the sand pit to the other! These resources don't break, they don't bend and they can withstand any man (child) handling, mistreatment or total disregard for it, as a piece of nursery equipment!

A IS FOR **AUTHENTIC MATERIALS**

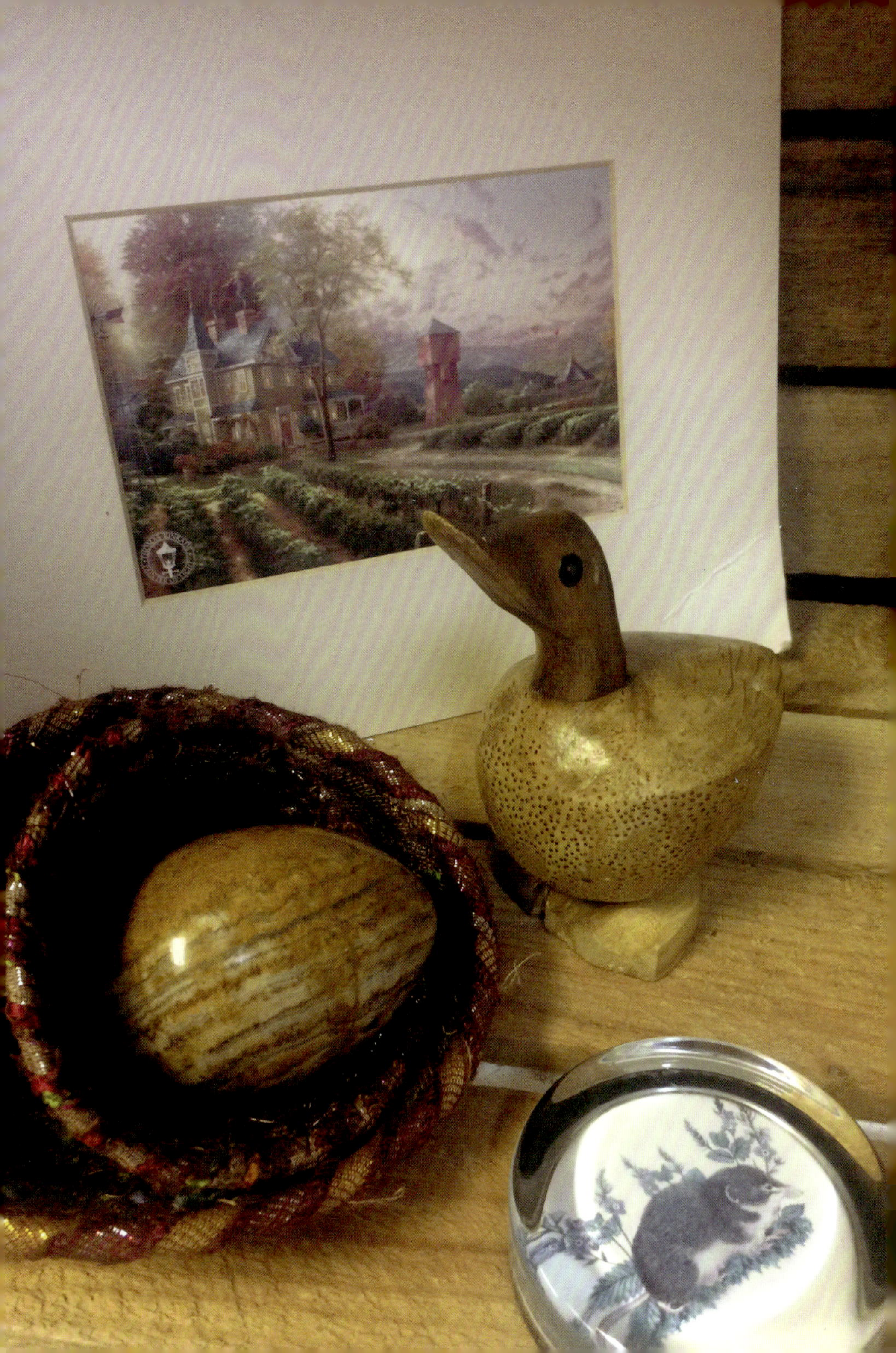

What messages are we giving our children, when everything we allow them to play with is PRETEND and an unbreakable resource? A child loves to mimic and replicate the actions of their loved ones, they want to re-enact real life scenarios and be like Mummy, Daddy or significant adults, peers etc.

So why is it we give them miniature, child sized replicas of the real thing? Why do we fob them off with tiny resources of unrealistic colours, patterns or designs? Aren't we undervaluing their play as just PRETEND? Aren't we sending messages to them that their play isn't real, therefore it's not worth giving them the 'good stuff'?

Children love to have what we have, they want the REAL mobile phone or TV remote. They can't be fooled with replacements and get frustrated when we try to offer them up instead! Who are we trying to kid? These children are smart cookies! So what's stopping you from allowing these items in your settings?

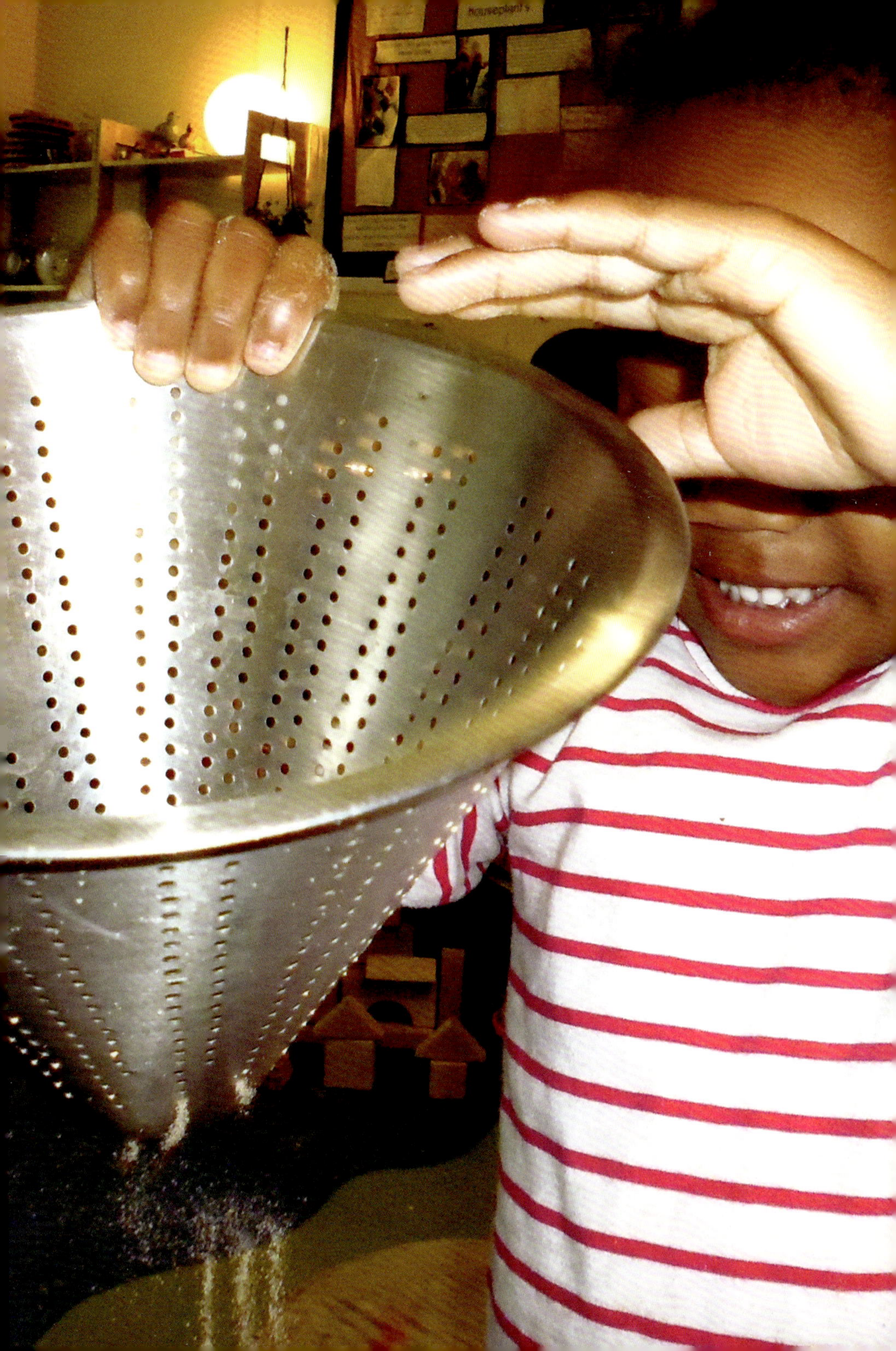

B

BEAUTY IS A DEEP HUMAN NEED

Beauty is innate within us all. Young children are very aware of this and are drawn to it! The resources and presentation that we offer within our settings should reflect beauty; from the delicate authentic resources to the wondrous natural objects – all declaring, all showing their beauty!

Create enchanted pockets of learning that have a visually appealing manner which highlight the magic, wonder and possibilities of the resources on offer, inviting the children to become curious about them.

As educators we should always be seeking to encourage the child's natural sense of wonder and love of beauty. Seek to create a place of many beauties, but most importantly the beauty of a childhood being lived to its potential. A beauty that is indeed deep in the eye of the beholder.

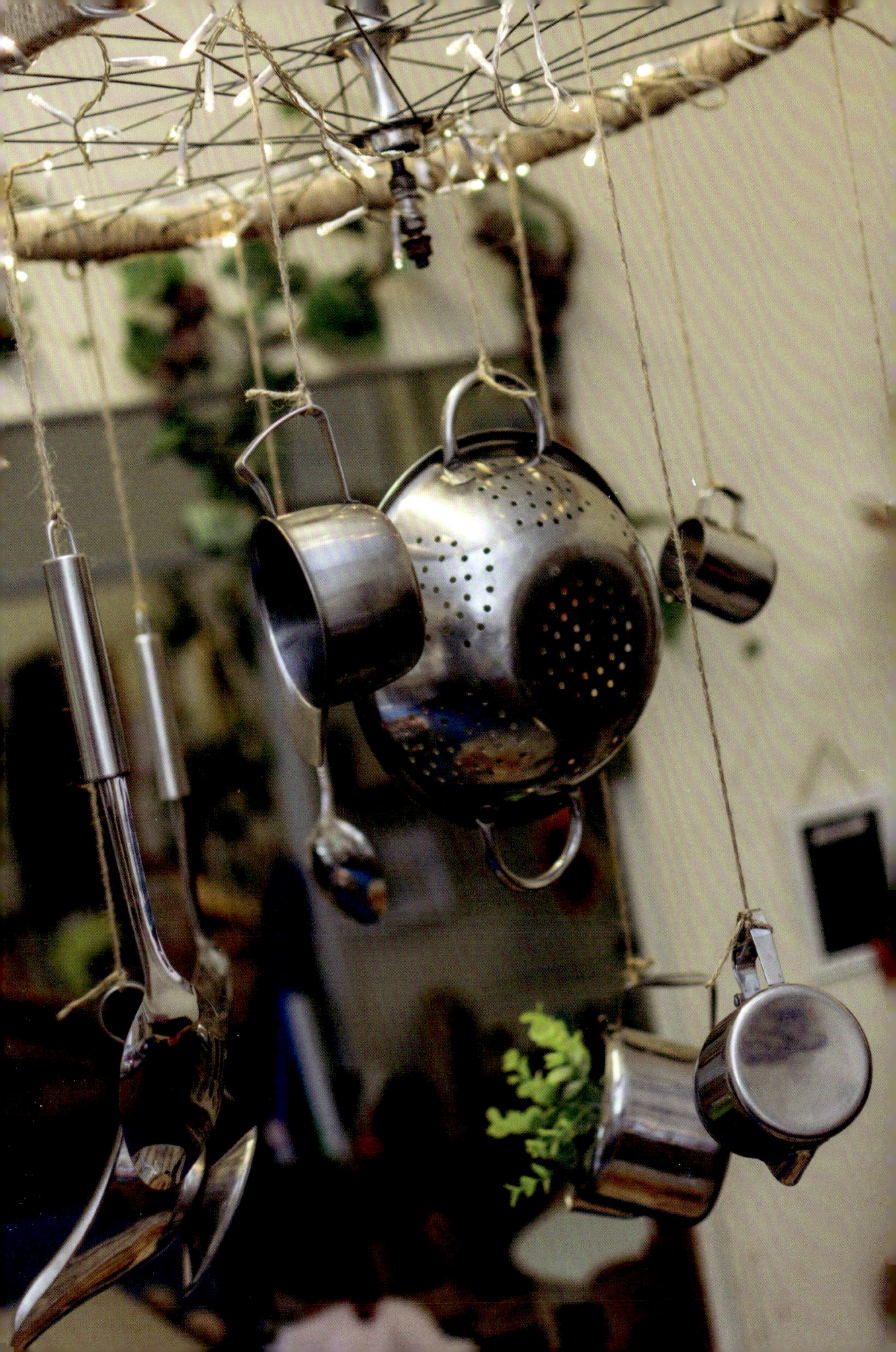

Curiosity
noun | *cu·ri·os·i·ty* | /kjʊərɪˈɒsɪti/
A strong desire to know or learn something.

CURIOUS MINDS

We are all born with the innate skill of curiosity, that strong desire is there, present in the baby from birth.

It is our job as early childhood educators to inspire and nurture an inquisitive mind in every child. It can be easily achieved from the environment we create to the questions we ask.

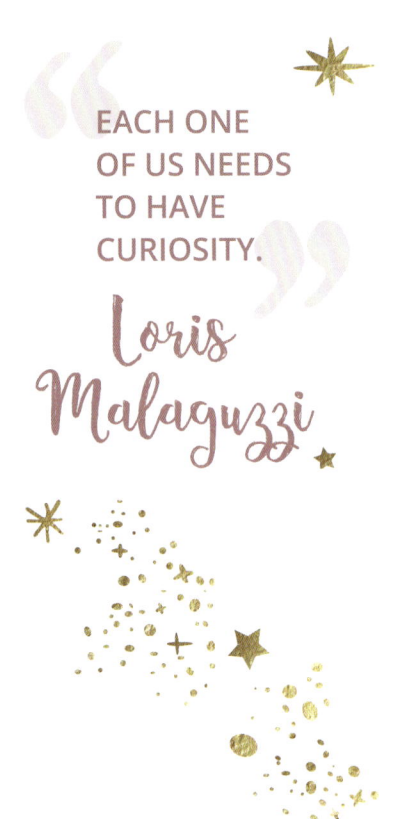

> **EACH ONE OF US NEEDS TO HAVE CURIOSITY.**
>
> *Loris Malaguzzi*

However, Doctor Bruce Perry tells us about three common ways adults can crush the curious child's learning: fear, disapproval and absence. A fearful child will be unwilling to explore and be curious, preferring to seek the familiar over anything new. The constant "don't touch", "don't climb", "don't do that", disapproval that children hear from the adult so often can also diminish the child's willingness to be curious.

With the absence of an invested adult, the child may not be as curious without that boundary of safety and someone to share in the discovery and joyfulness of learning with the child. So, lessons for us all as educators: be present, be curious, have fun and really make a difference!

Quote source: Your Image of the Child - Where Teaching Begins (1993).

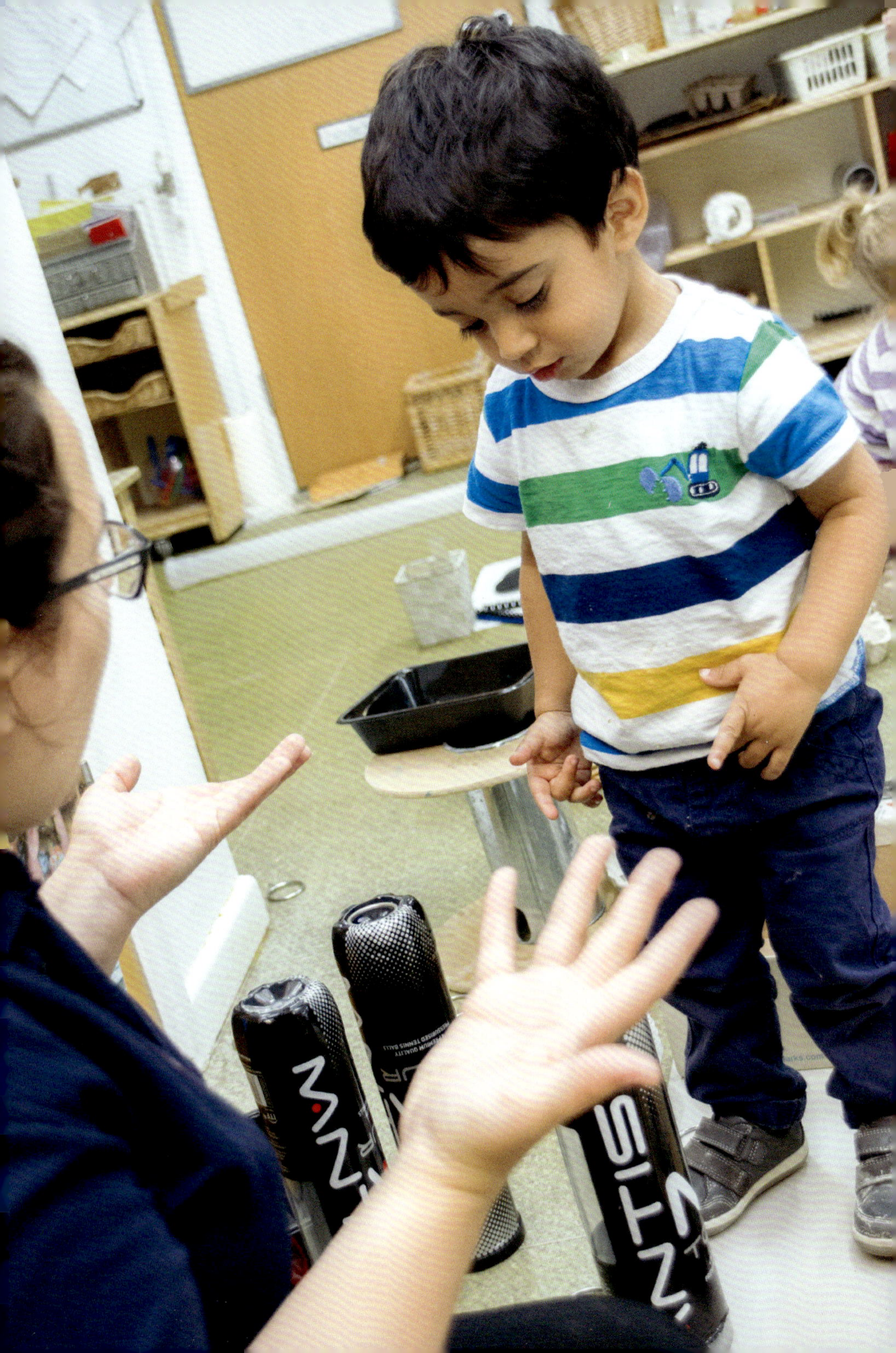

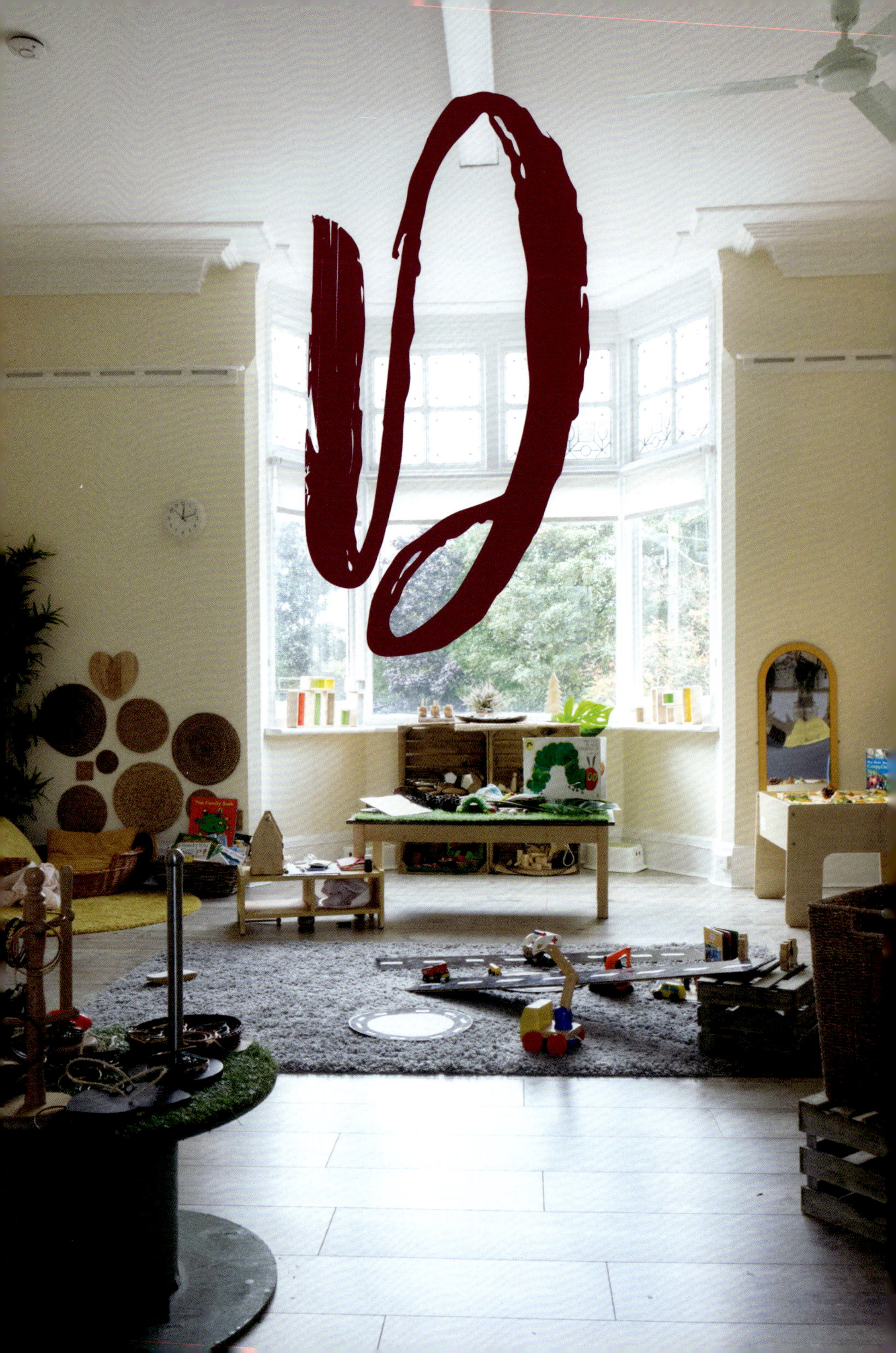

DISPLAY

We are advocates for calm, neutral backgrounds for any displays, to let learning shine through, making it become visible! But also we do this to create a sense of calmness without over stimulating those who it is intended for – the children!

Researchers at Carnigie Mellon in Pittsburgh studied the impact of brightly decorated early childhood establishments on 'distractibility' and discovered that bright visual displays can actually have a negative impact on learning in young children.

At The Curiosity Approach® we promote the use of natural, earthy tones on your walls to radiate a sense of calmness. Colour plays an important role in the overall aesthetic of a space, it can also impact an individual's mood, emotional wellbeing, learning and behaviour.

Within a Steiner Waldorf school there is a deliberate and conscious use of colour on the walls; generally soft warm pink tones are used because of their gently active and supportive quality. They also incorporate objects from nature into their displays bringing the seasons into them.

Careful consideration should be given to making your displays into a visible trace of the children's thinking and learning – process rather than product. We are also huge advocates of displays that honour a child's family and home life, communicating a powerful message of being and belonging. You will always find family displayed within our settings.

D IS FOR **DISPLAY**

Thought and care should go into every display within your setting from a wall display to a provocation for learning ensuring that they are not excessive and the use of colour has a positive impact rather than an overpowering one. Within our settings you will always see natural light, less decoration and more natural materials.

ENCHANTING ENVIRONMENTS

Magic and fairy tales, awe and wonder have always been a huge interest of young children around the world. Lost in the imaginary world, mesmerized and excited by the thought of fantasy and make believe – stories of the Tooth Fairy, mermaids and Santa. Fairy tales and magical make believe have enchanted us throughout the centuries, from traditional fables to modern day examples such as JK Rowling, author of the Harry Potter series.

Children engaging with the wonder of their own incredible imaginations, storytelling and role play and this is carefully encouraged through thoughtful provocations and environments that have an air of mystery and magic.

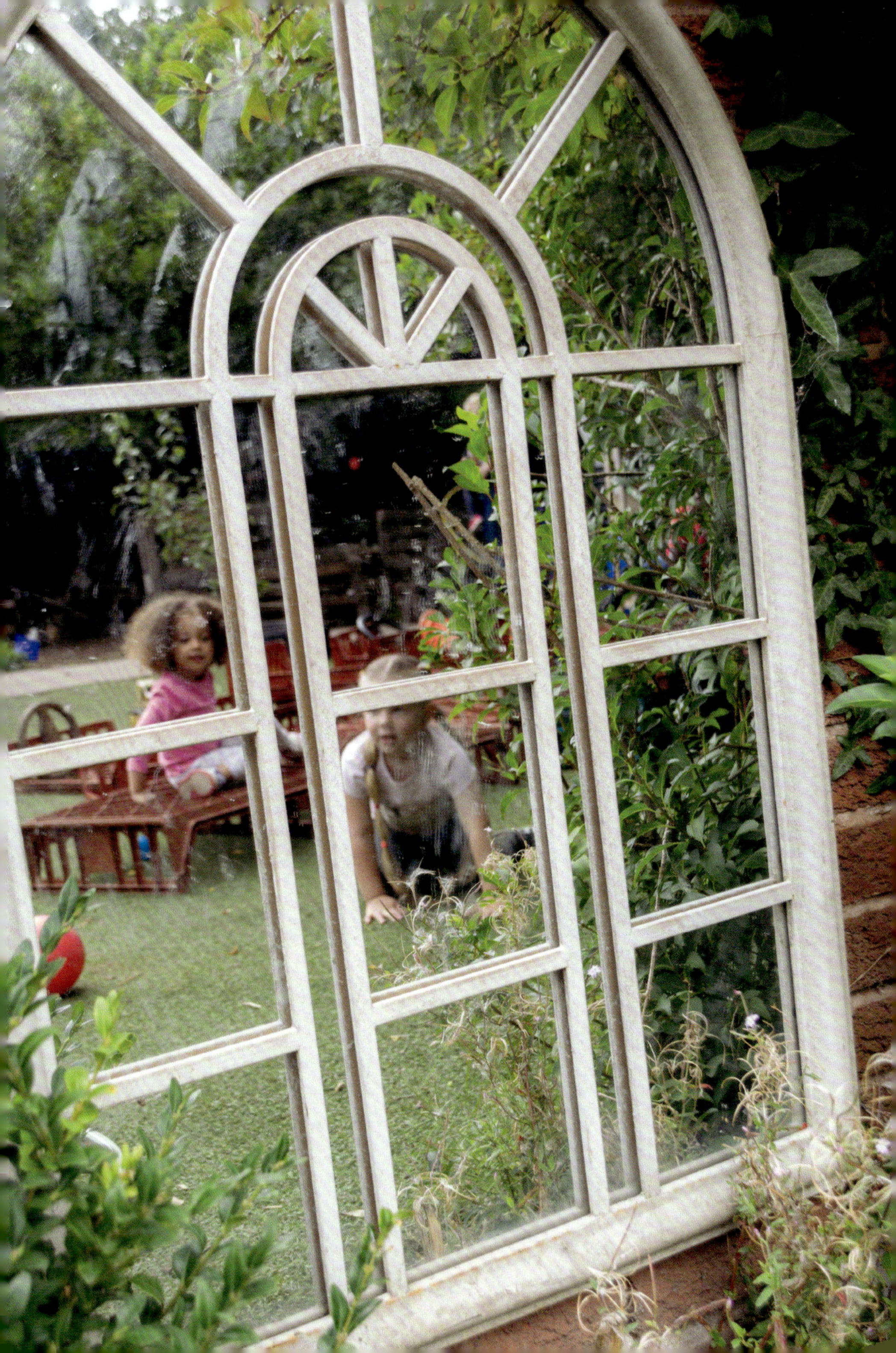

Every area of a Curiosity Approach setting from the main entrance, cloak rooms and toilets to children's main play spaces are respected and cared for. With calm, neutral tones and intriguing artifacts and displays, children feel they are entering a beautiful magical space where they feel relaxed, welcomed and at home. Mirrors, fairy lights and attention to detail are all part of The Curiosity Approach®, these offer a touch of magic in what could have traditionally been an institutionalised and over stimulating environment.

E IS FOR **ENCHANTING ENVIRONMENTS**

Within each setting, adults will thoughtfully present resources, sending subliminal messages to children. Adults are passionate about their environments and seek to offer incredible opportunities to children, opening that mystical door to endless possibilities and the journey into a child's incredible imagination. The outcomes are limitless if we as adults value the play space we provide. Take care of the most valuable part of our team, the environment. Treat her as our 'best friend', look after her and ensure that she is respected.

Take time to teach children to respect the resources and their play spaces, teach them the value of resources, items, people and things. How are children going to grow and respect our amazing incredible planet if the only resources and equipment they encounter is disposable, indestructible plastic or a wealth of mixed up unloved and broken toys.

By providing magical enchanted play spaces for children, you are providing them with the opportunity to get lost in their own imagination, to be free from constraints of the modern educational system. Their imagination has no rules or boundaries, no right or wrong way to play, act or behave. In a child's mind, they can be whoever they want to be, resources can be anything their heart desires and their creativity skills are given the freedom to expand and develop to new heights well beyond their academic years.

The enchanted environment isn't solely just for the child, if we can ignite the passion and excitement within adults to create purposeful and enabling environments, then surely this is a positive step forward.

Adults will see the magic awe and wonder though the eyes of a child, releasing that inner playfulness that sadly has been locked away. Conditioned to believe that fairies no longer exist. Allowing staff/adults to feel empowered and courageous, to laugh and be silly, to have fun and pretend.

By setting up beautiful play spaces for children, we are giving adults permission to be young again, to use the most amazing resources they have within their setting, themselves! Confident playful researchers who offload the baggage of self-consciousness and return to that magical awe-inspiring world of make believe and pretend.

Release the inner child within and emerge into a world of curiosity awe and wonder. Let the learning begin with the heart and everything will fit beautifully into place.

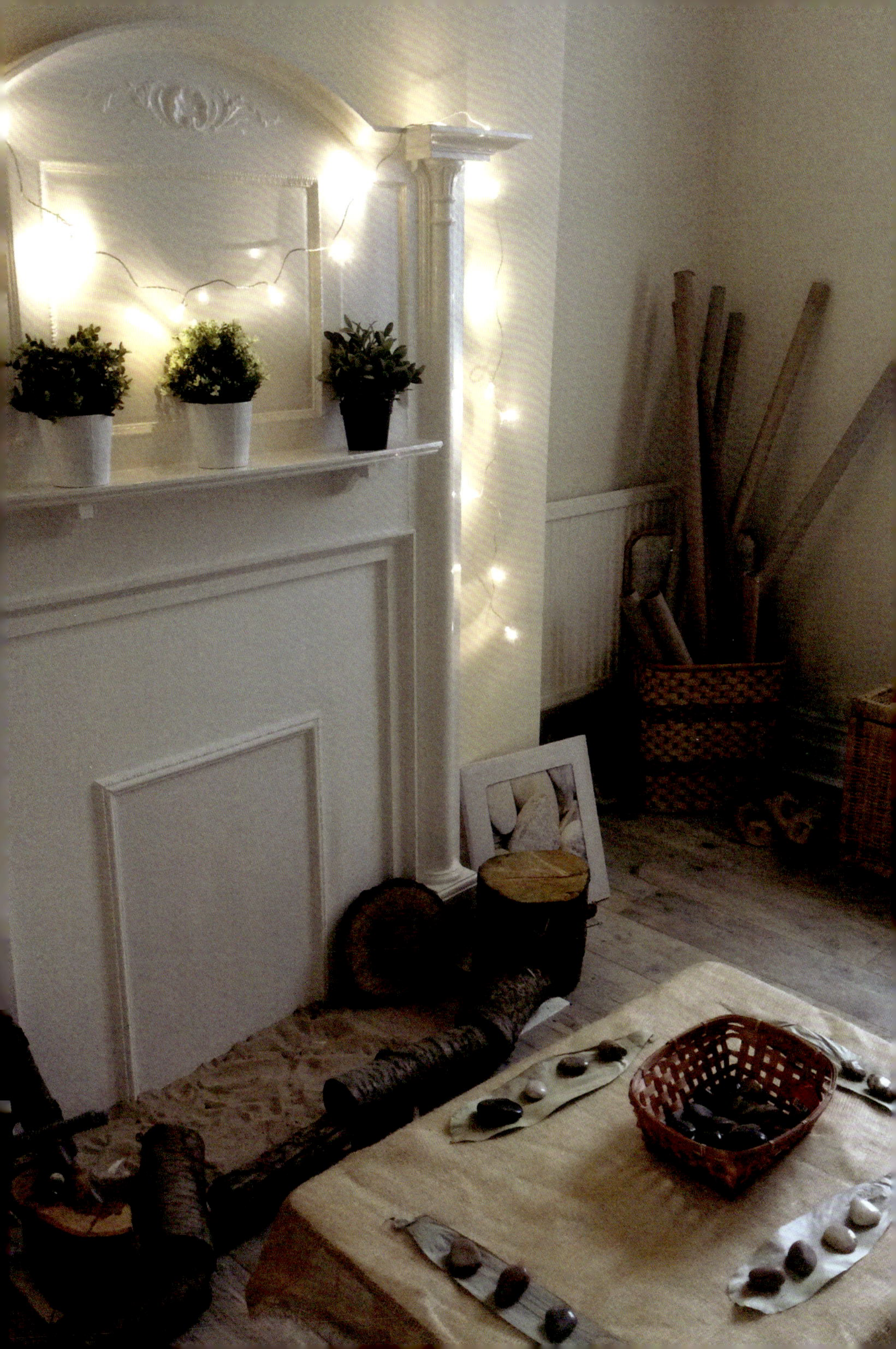

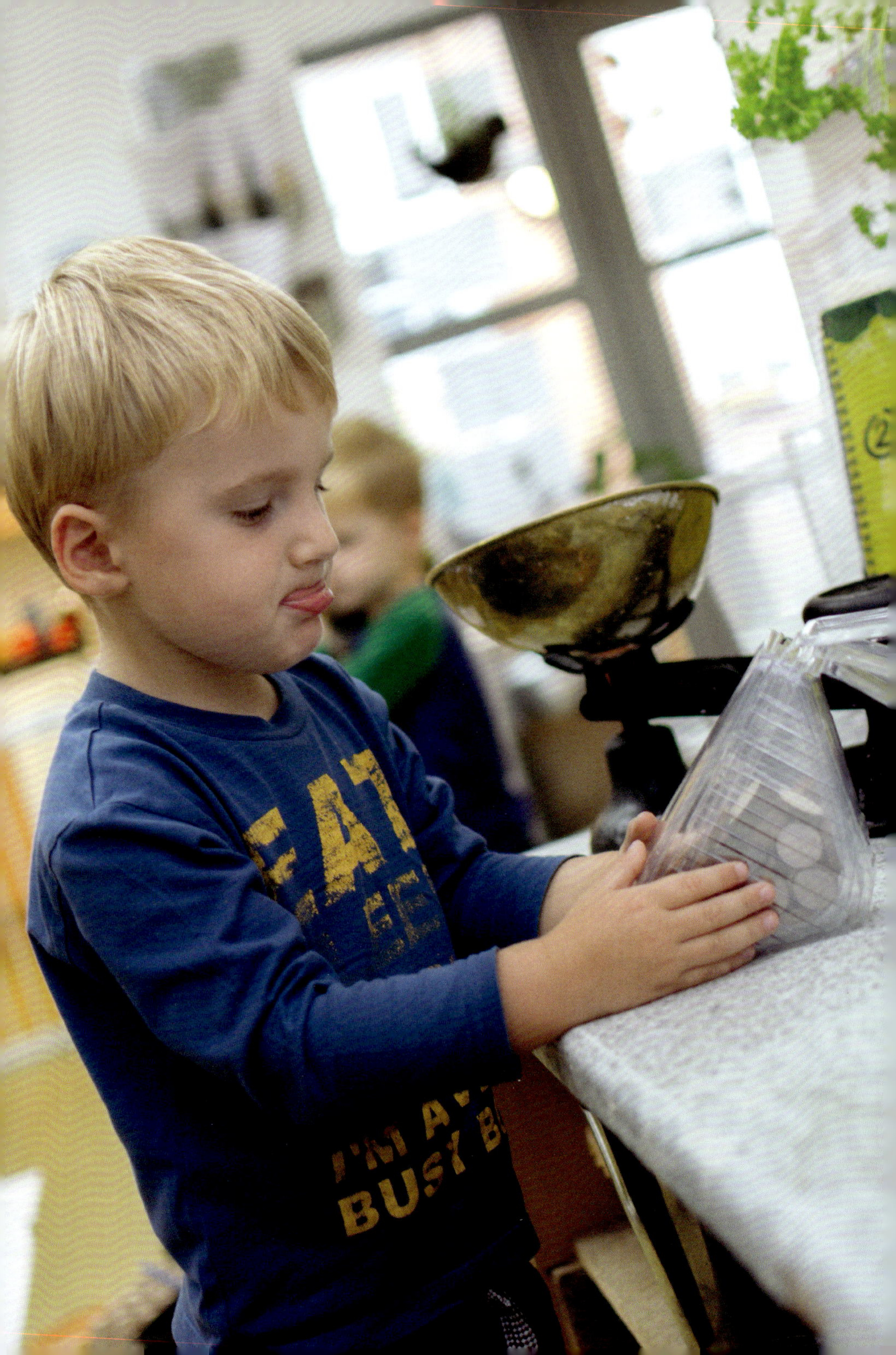
BUSY

FUTURE

Modern day toys tell children how to play with them; they resemble something so closely that it becomes difficult for children to use them in any way other than their purpose. A plastic toy car, for example, is almost always going to be a car, then add in elements of technology and we find we are drastically reducing the innate skills of curiosity within our children.

Inquisitiveness, deep level thinking, communication and social skills are also declining, as children spend large proportions of time with their head fixed to a screen. We know that a child learns through the five senses, wanting to touch everything and get into everything so they can figure out and learn about the world around them. If these senses become fully occupied by technology, for some children, they start to ignore the world around them. Not wanting to splash in a puddle or get their hands dirty in mud, missing the bumble bee buzzing past them – these wondrous things sadly become lost on the young child.

As educators, we play a significant role in protecting the skills of the next generation, the future! And there are many benefits to technology but the balance needs to be right. Remember, so many children when they leave the setting each day, will have screen time, so how necessary is it in your setting? How many other ways can you provide technology that can ignite curiosity and further learning?

Getting the learning environment right will help take significant leaps in protecting and embedding these innate skills. Think about the modern toys you may have and question how much do they allow for imagination, curiosity, awe and wonder?

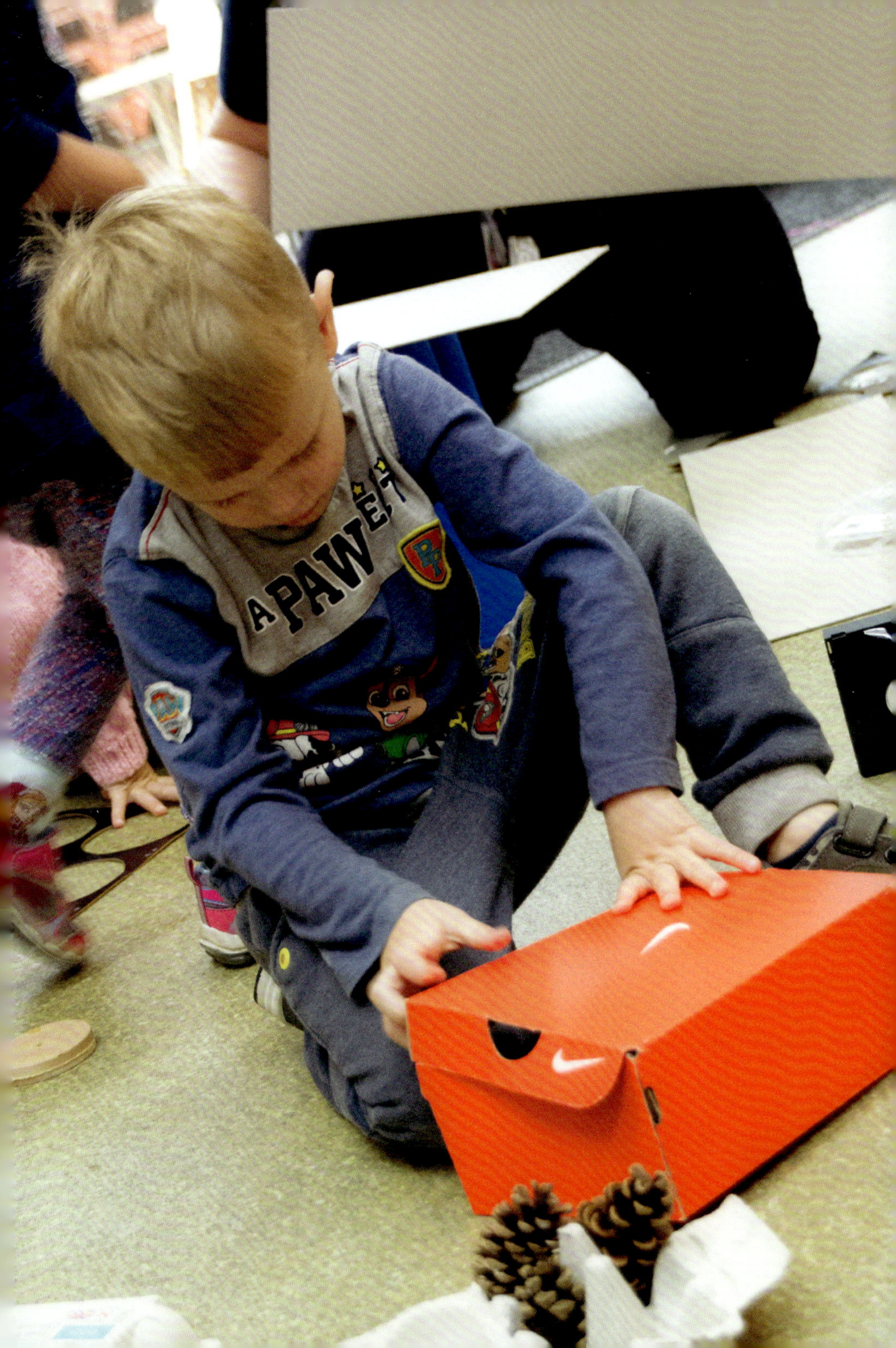

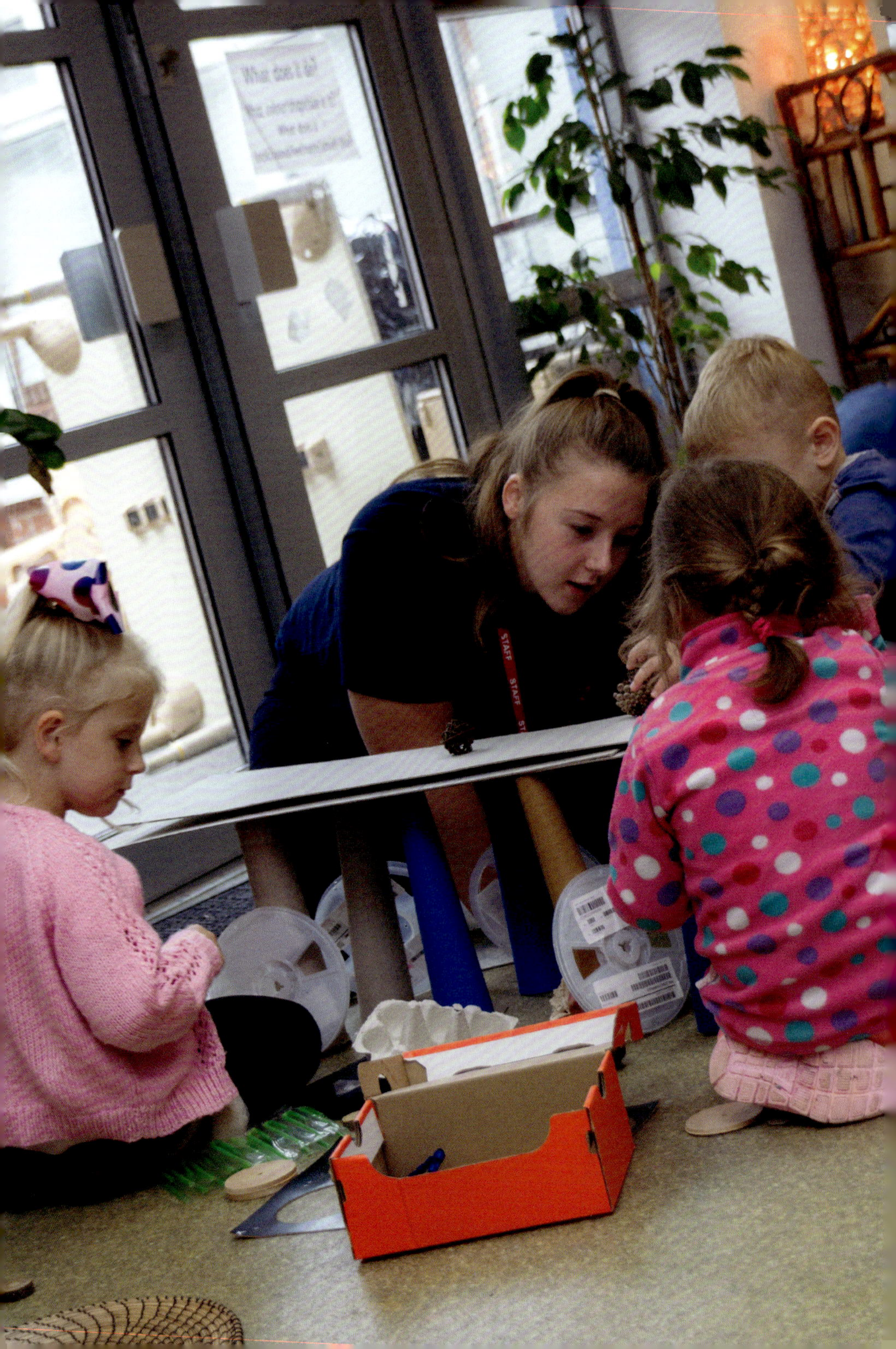
STAFF

GLOBAL INSPIRATION

Steiner Waldorf, Reggio Emilia and Te Whãriki are the three progressive approaches to early childhood education that set the foundations to The Curiosity Approach®. Over the years we have become captivated by key pedagogical elements from each approach, together they form The Curiosity Approach®.

Rudolf Steiner was an Austrian philosopher whose works form the foundation of the Waldorf education program in the late nineteenth century. His philosophies teach us that spiritiual experiences are essential for the development of happy, confident young children. He regularly spoke of the importance of love and warmth, joy, creativity, gratitude and respect for the environment. His remarkable teachings have influenced our own approach.

Loris Malaguzzi was a teacher whose revolutionary methods have attracted education professionals from across the world to the town of Reggio Emilia in Northern Italy. Whilst so many of the Reggio principles are embraced within The Curiosity Approach®, one that stands out as key is that there are three effective 'teachers' of children – adults, other children and their physical environment, with the latter commonly referred to as the 'third teacher'. The approach requires children to be seen as competent, resourceful, imaginative, inventive and curious – those who possess a desire to interact and communicate with others around them. This book is filled with joyous images of how we embed the Reggio Emila methods within our own settings.

G IS FOR **GLOBAL INSPIRATION**

Background image ID 84065420 © Andreykuzmin | Dreamstime

Te Whāriki originates in New Zealand. It is the principles and curriculum set out by the Ministry of Education to be used in early childhood. The words 'Te Whāriki' are Maori for 'woven mat'. The vision is founded upon the following aspirations for children: "to grow up as competent and confident learners and communicators, healthy in mind, body, and spirit, secure in their sense of belonging and in the knowledge that they make a valued contribution to society."

It is the deep well-being of the child that is an overarching principle of The Curiosity Approach® and the idea that children interact completely with their environment and everywhere is a learning environment.

Together they all provide a canvas for imagination, creativity and curiosity to flourish, they are The Curiosity Approach®.

Quote source: Te Whariki published 2017 by the Ministry of Education, New Zealand, copyright © Crown. Full version available at http://tewhariki.tki.org.nz/en/early-childhood-curriculum-document

Hygge

hue-gah

A quality of cosiness and comfortable conviviality that engenders a feeling of contentment or well-being (regarded as a defining characteristic of Danish culture).

Oxford Dictionary

HOMELY HYGGE

Hygge is a Danish word used when acknowledging a feeling or moment, ordinary or extraordinary as cosy, charming or special. Curiosity Approach settings would seek to create an environment that captures that feeling of cosiness, warmth and togetherness for all who enter into it. To have a deep sense of atmosphere, creating a feeling of 'home' throughout your early childhood environment – creating an extension of the family home rather than a watered down version of a school, for a school is not the place for our youngest children.

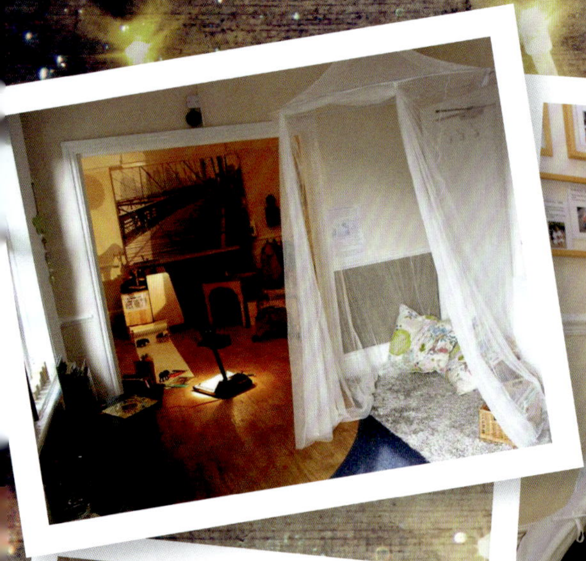
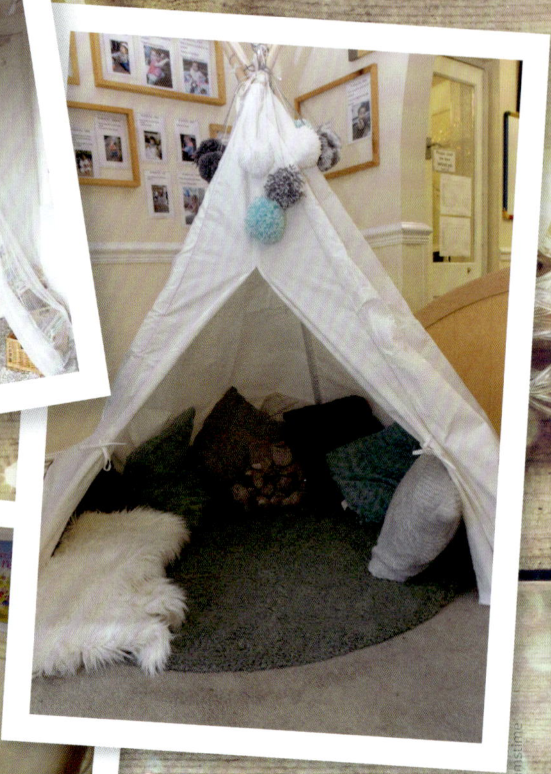
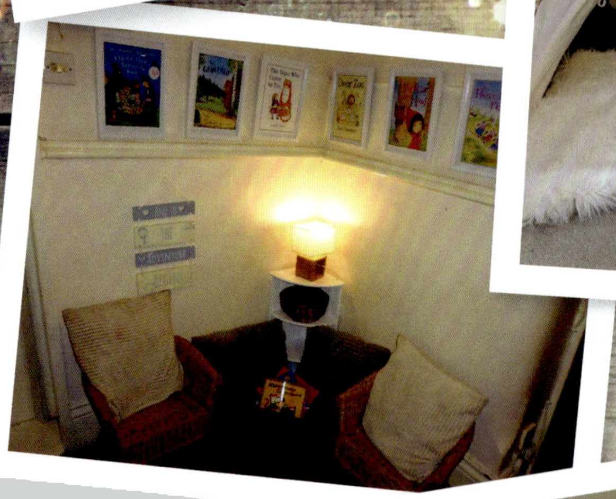
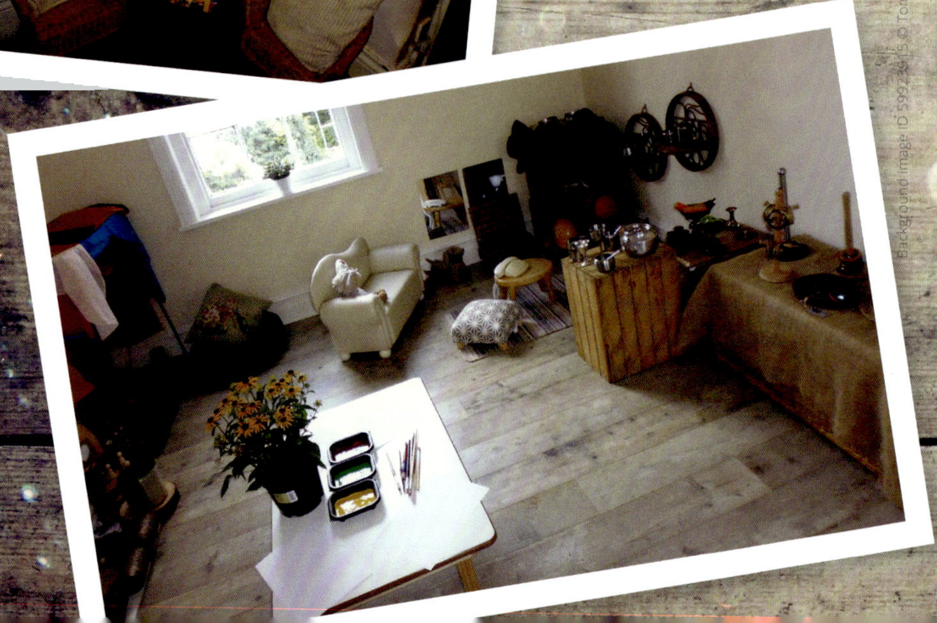

That hygge feeling can be created in early childhood settings in so many different ways; from the strong relationships to the delicate lighting, layering textures comfortable for cosy times, creating 'den' spaces full of comfort and softness where a child can enjoy time together with a friend or alone time, adding warmth to your space through natural elements such as plants and wood, eating together, singing together, sharing a story together… the possibilities are endless.

Sit on the floor in your setting, see it from the eyes and height of the child – how does it feel? Is the floor hard and cold? Is there a draft blowing in, unnoticed at the adult height? Is it cosy down there? If not, make the change, bring the magic of hygge through your doors.

J

INVITATIONS TO LEARNING

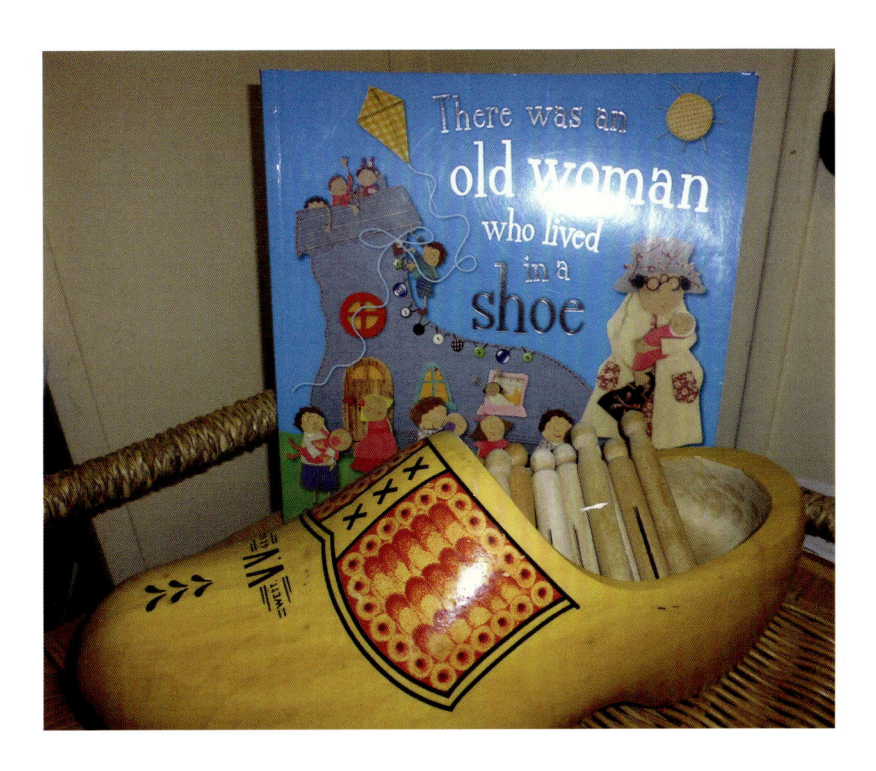

Within our nurseries we provide thoughtful invitations to learning: provocations which inspire children to come and play, to draw children in with subliminal messages and invitations to explore, to be curious and inquisitive.

Staff carefully set up invitations following on from a child's initial line of enquiry and interest. It isn't about what the adult wants to provide or what adults think looks nice, inviting or beautiful. This needs to reflect on a child's interest or learning style, it needs to extend the learning that previously happened. Like a game of ping pong, the adult needs to keep the interest alive with further opportunities to learn and develop.

Children have no idea of the wealth of activities available or the endless possibilities to play. Children need a little prompt, to provoke a thought or idea.

Create beautiful spaces or activities with thoughtful purpose, leaving room for children to extend and play. Create too much and there will be no room for the children to add or extend. Leave them with the desire to engage in deep levels of learning and critical thinking.

Provide children with a range of resources. If setting up an art provocation, use books and photographs which offer reference to the subject matter. An opportunity for children to be researchers in their own learning. Provide a range of brushes which allow children to select independently, colours that can be mixed, stirred and transformed into exquisite art work.

When resources are set up with care and attention they will encourage children to settle, to play, engage longer and prevents them flitting from one activity to another. Children's attention spans increase and develop as they are nurtured through these carefully thought out invitations to learn. Children's natural curiosity is ignited and their excitement to play and engage is inspired. It's incredible to watch as children become fully, deeply absorbed in a play space invited into their own magical land of imagination, awe and wonder.

WITH A MIRROR THAT MAKES
YOU PART OF THE BOOK!

DB.1

Small world animals and figures can be used to extend the learning and to ensure children's interests are incorporated. Natural resources, plants and log slices offer a base for any provocation. Bring elements of nature to each learning opportunity, mixed thoughtfully with loose parts, which children can use an adapt to meet their own deep critical thinking, creativity and magical ideas.

Encourage passionate staff to be researchers in their own professional development, to seek out ideas to setting up activities and those gentle invites to come and play.

49

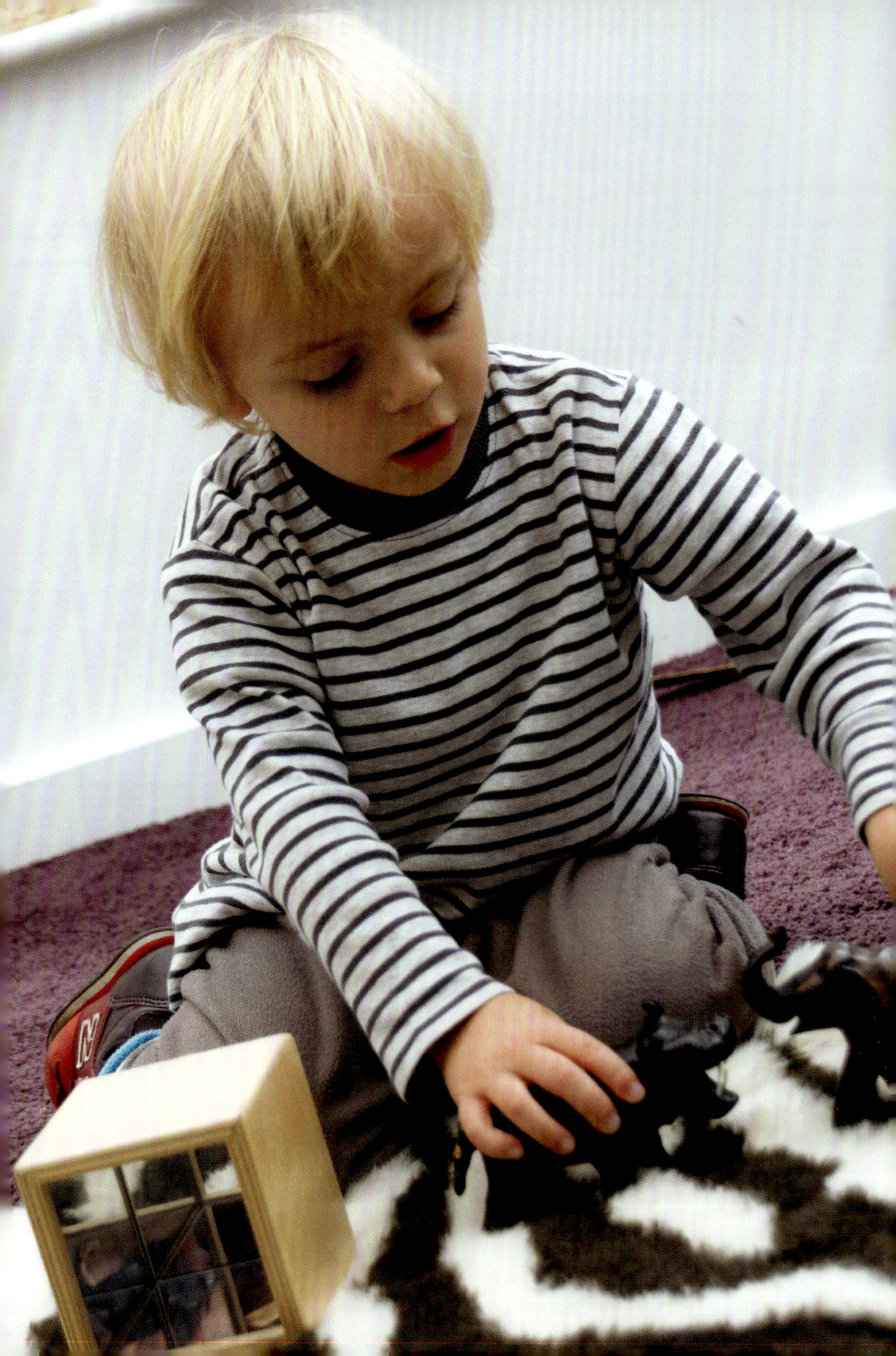

J

JOY OF LEARNING

51

Curiosity, or that eager desire to know, is the key to the joy of learning. Children's curious minds are open and flexible and their hearts trusting and generous, ready to be filled will the joy of learning.

Children learn through imitation, so if we want to create a culture of purposeful joyful learning within our settings then this behaviour must be modelled to our wonderful little people. As early childhood educators we should demonstrate actions that would be worthy of imitation and filled with purposeful joy. Our role as an educator is to find what interests the child and provide them with opportunities to explore these interests further.

J IS FOR **JOY OF LEARNING**

How do you create a joyful learning environment? In his book 'Places for Babies', Jim Greenman describes just how that setting should be. He speaks of roomed filled with lots of natural light with shadows 'dancing' on the walls and floors and of a range of furniture for children discover texture, shape and size – and well as the physical over, under, around and of course, in. He makes reference to cosy, calm nooks and also to the essential access to opportunities to freely explore a selection of 'sensuous' substances while making a wild mess! He talks about how an early childhood setting should be just like a child's house, with separate places that sound, smell, look and feel different from each other - just like their rooms at home.

Now that is a joyful Curiosity Approach setting – can you create an amazing environment like that?

KINAESTHETIC LEARNERS

Kinaesthetic learners are those of us who prefer using our bodies, hands and sense of touch to learn. You'll agree – bet you have an environment full of them!

Children in the first few years of life are building neurological pathways in their brains faster than they ever will again in their life span. They are so full of energy because they are working in overdrive trying to absorb as much learning as they can both physically and mentally. That is why they can be amazingly exhausting!

Kinaesthetic learners are those children who surpass in finding out things for themselves without any need for real guidance. They love tinkering, finding out how things work and being physical. The world just feels like a giant playground full of wonderful things to discover and explore for our kinaesthetic learners.

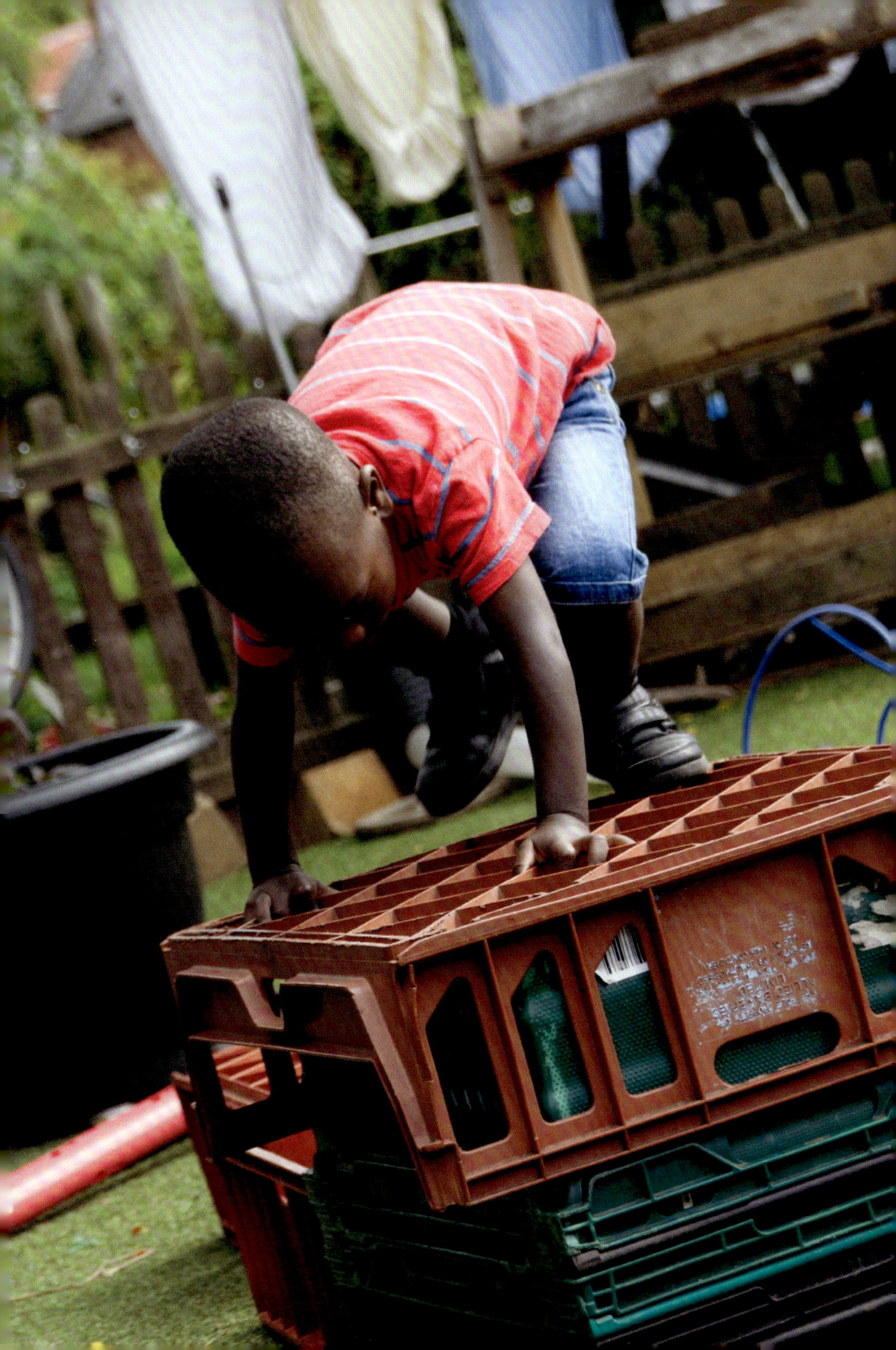

K IS FOR **KINESTHETIC LEARNERS**

Pretty much most young children benefit from having a kinesthetic environment to learn in – one where touching, feeling, experiencing is fully allowed and embraced. Again, in this digital world we are leading a more sedentary lifestyle, one that we are offering and modelling to our children, where screen time amounts to hours through a day for some children it is so important we offer a rich environment full of copious opportunities to learn both physically and mentally. Are you offering plenty of outdoor time? Are you adding movement to story times? Our young children need to be constantly moving and exploring. Not only is movement important for brain development and the growing mind, it also helps promote health and reduces anxiety.

L

LOOSE PARTS

The concept of loose parts has been around for forever or however long children have played with sticks and stones! The theory of loose parts was created in 1971 by an architect named Simon Nicholson.

Nicholson criticised how children were always presented with finished materials, resources and environments that did not allow for any imagination. He believed that all children are creative beings and that this should be nurtured not robbed! His solution, the way to nurture children's creativity was to give them loose parts and they have delighted us since. Community Playthings in 2014 described them as 'the opposite of toys'. Nicholson said that toys are items that have a specific purpose –loose parts do not, they are what children want them to be.

Loose parts can be natural or man-made items that can be used in a multitude of ways with no pre-designed outcome. Children can combine them, line them up, join them together, transport them etc. Having 'loose parts' available in a play space allows children to use these materials as they choose. Once children awaken to the potential of loose parts they are developing opportunities for creativity, critical thinking, problem-solving, counting and sorting to name but a few, teaching children how to think and not what to think!

L IS FOR **LOOSE PARTS**

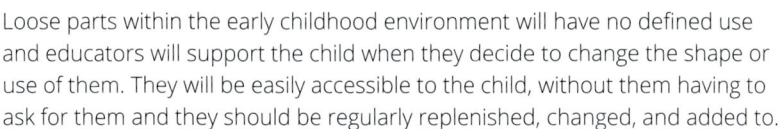

Loose parts within the early childhood environment will have no defined use and educators will support the child when they decide to change the shape or use of them. They will be easily accessible to the child, without them having to ask for them and they should be regularly replenished, changed, and added to.

When children use 'loose parts' it can be anything their amazing minds imagine it to be but you can bet it will be with purpose! Let their imagination be everywhere...

L IS FOR **LOOSE PARTS**

> "THE WIDER THE RANGE OF POSSIBILITIES WE OFFER CHILDREN, THE MORE INTENSE WILL BE THEIR MOTIVATIONS AND THE RICHER THEIR EXPERIENCES."
>
> *Loris Malaguzzi*

Quote source: p79, *The hundred languages of children: The Reggio Emilia approach – Advanced reflections* (2000)

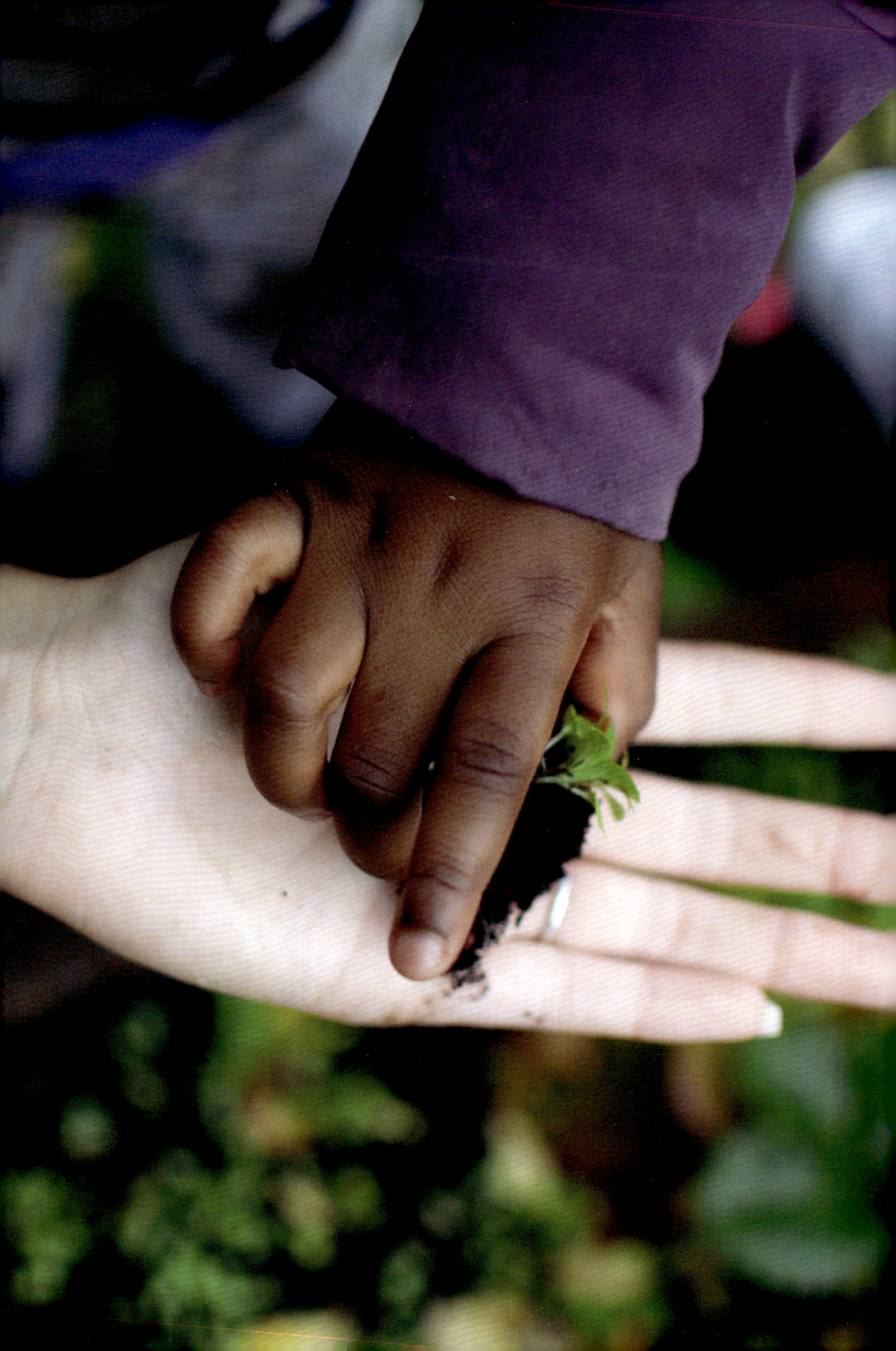

MINDFULNESS

As part of our approach we believe that mindfulness is hugely important, to always be aware of what is happening in the here and now! This also links beautifully with the planning process of 'in the moment planning'.

To look and actually see, appreciating the amazing learning that is happening right at that particular moment in time.

As educators, we also need to ensure that we are mindful of our own mindset and the effects it has on our young children – to greet each day as a new beginning, to go to work with a positive mental attitude and see the positive in all the amazing opportunities around us.

Only through being thoughtful, curious and passionate practitioners can we hope to inspire these incredible little learners. We have a huge responsibility and have been blessed with an incredible gift. To be in charge of these little ones, who look to us for attention, guidance and inspiration. We are their role models; therefore we need to be excited about the wonderful day ahead. To leave our emotional baggage at the door and to work with a positive mental attitude to each day.

As stated in Reggio Emilia settings, we need to be the researchers alongside children, we need to see the world through the eyes of a child and seek out the magic and wonder in all we see.

To ensure our little children remain curious and inquisitive about the natural world, as adults we need to regain our own feelings of wonder and awe. To slow down and revisit feeling from our youth. Gain back our own excitement at making discoveries, to nurture our children and join them on this magical journey of curiosity awe and wonder. How can we do this? We believe the main thing to do is to play with young children, relax and regain our own childhood skills that we believe have been lost. Shake off those negative messages that have been laid down over time, those sub modalities that subconsciously prevent us from playing freely or making us feel self-conscious and insecure. Allow ourselves to explore, be adventurous, have the confidence to give things a
go – even if we feel nervous or uncertain. Take a leaf out of these children's books – live life to the full and see the pleasure and enjoyment in everything we do.

We spend a huge amount of time at work and therefore we need to belong, to build relationships with our team, our tribe and to share ideas, thinking and celebrate our achievements.

Throughout a Curiosity Approach setting inspirational quotes are everywhere, staff are also encouraged to share their favourite quotes and the words that resonate highly with them.

Mindfulness is about stepping away from negative energy, making the emotional space for children calm, relaxed healthy and beautiful. To appreciate the tiny things in life, whether this be the raindrops on your tongue on a wet miserable day or the gentle hug given to a child who is looking for reassurance.

MINDFULNESS TAKES PRACTICE, MINDFULNESS TAKES TIME.

Sometimes in a busy, hectic setting it can be tricky to remind ourselves to wait, step back and appreciate the learning that is happening. To appreciate the incredible effort a child is showing when trying to put on their coat for the first time. To wait and allow a child time to listen and process their thinking and then answer, before we bulldoze in and talk for this incredible little learner.

Step back, be patient, be mindful of the magic that is happening... the deep levels of concentration and learning before our eyes.

N IS FOR **NATURAL MATERIALS**

NATURAL MATERIALS

An important aspect of our job is to teach our children to appreciate all that nature has to offer. Along with extended periods spent out in the outdoors, you should ensure that your environment is full of natural materials to fill the senses and ignite the flames of curiosity.

Nature offers us so many magical things that stimulate children's imagination and creativity, and cultivates curiosity, awe and wonder. The way we think about materials we bring into our settings can really reflect how we think about the children we serve; what are the children capable of? How will they connect with the materials? Natural materials are so open-ended their potential is limitless.

Natural materials should be an integral part of your environment and feature heavily within your loose parts play. They are open-ended, flexible and best of all each one is complexly unique, the perfect companion of loose parts! Children not only use them with intrigue, they use them to sort, match, count, order, construct with, the list really is endless! Each individual natural resource stimulates the senses in their own special way from the cool, hard stone to the prickly fir cone. Natural materials can be fluid and offered through sand, soil and water etc.

Woven in the threads of Te Whāriki children will learn about the features of their natural environment, and develop a sense of respect and responsibility for natural resources. It is without any doubt that using natural materials within your early childhood setting will certainly foster a sense of awe and wonder.

N IS FOR **NATURAL MATERIALS**

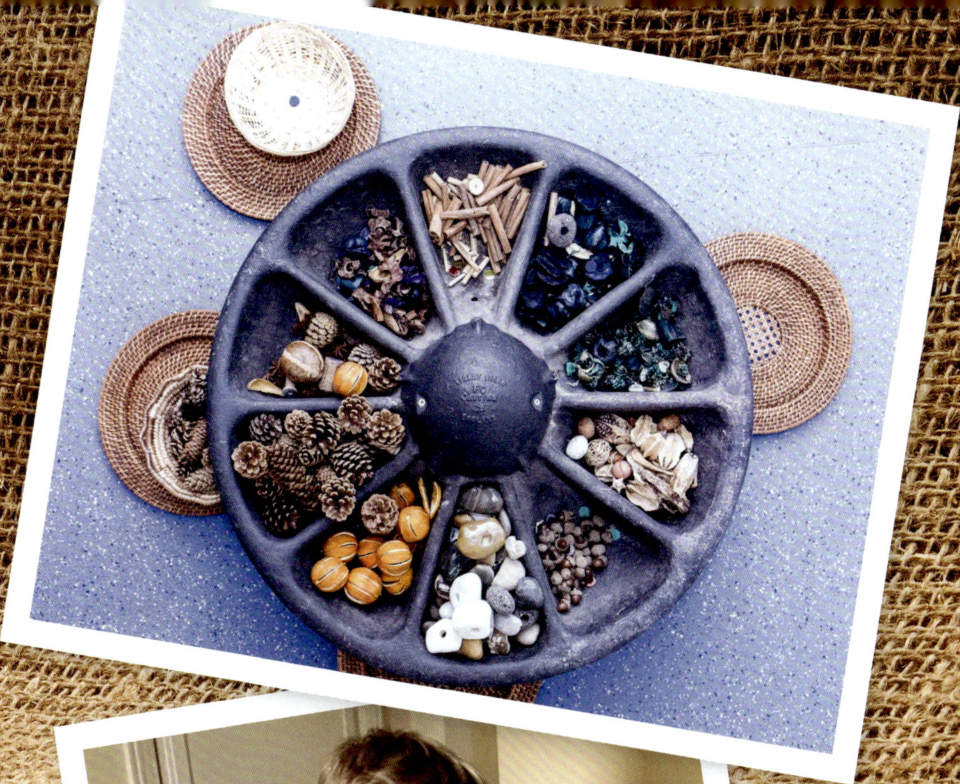

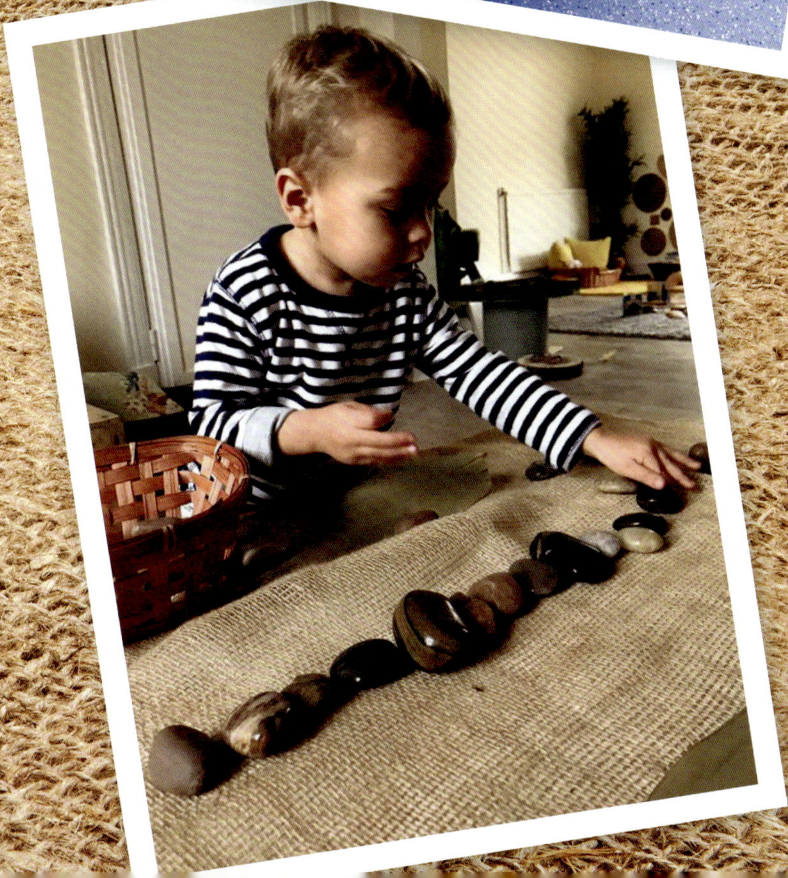

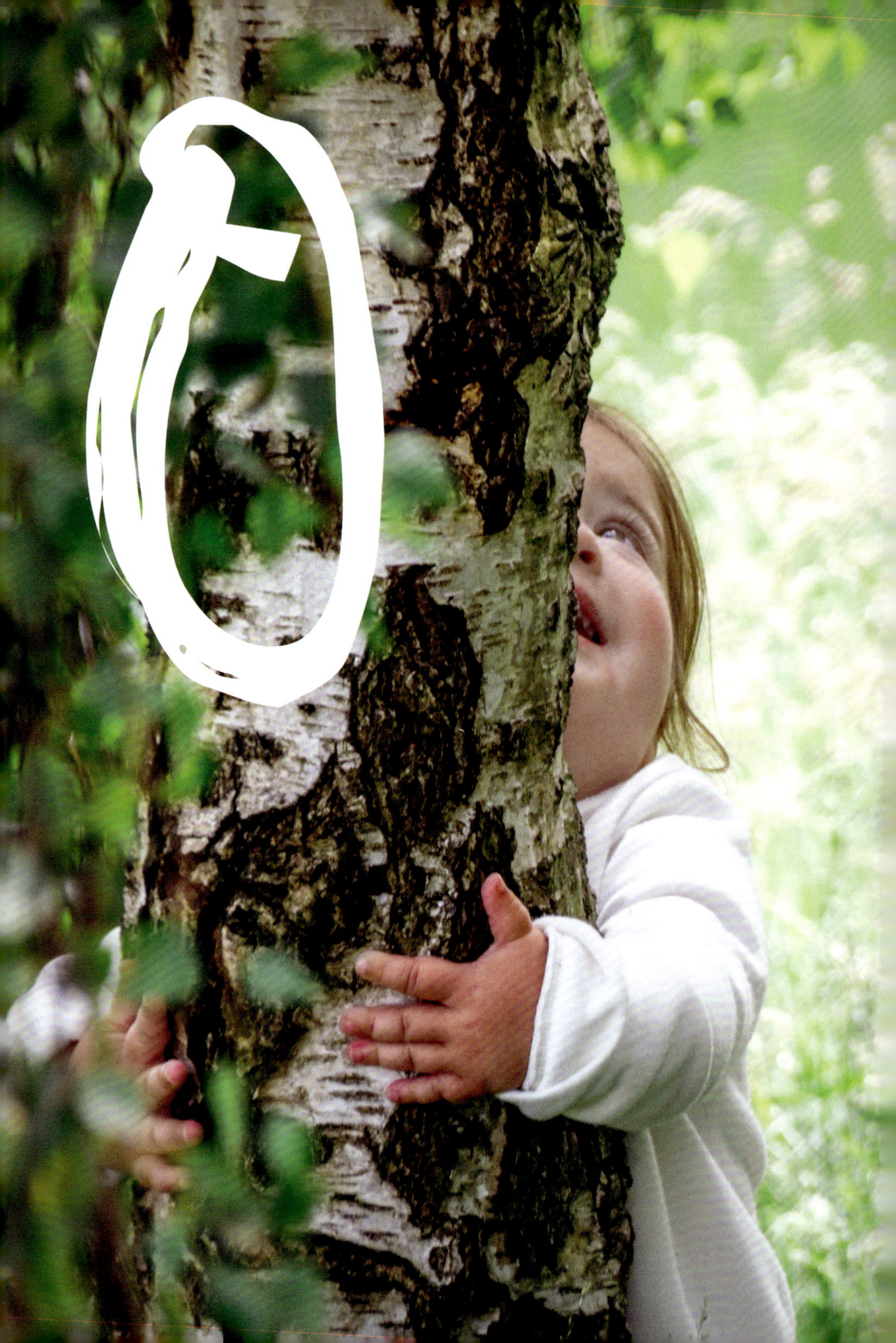

OPPORTUNITIES OUTDOORS

What an amazing world we live in, never lose sight of what surrounds you! Even if you open your doors onto concrete, you will find that tiny little ant scurrying by, the big old bird sitting high in the tree, the sun shining on your face or the wind blowing through your hair. It is essential that we give our children plentiful opportunities to spend lots of time outside.

No special equipment is ever needed in the outdoors. Mother Nature provides it all if you look carefully enough. Pause daily to notice the beautiful creations around us and model an example of gratitude and wonder for our children. Steiner teachings are that gratitude is the basis for love and when children deepen their appreciation for the natural world, they deepen their love for all of creation.

73

Children's sense of balance, touch and well-being are all nurtured by unhurried outdoor experiences.

Don't be perturbed by the weather, see the phenomena of the weather through the eyes of the child as something new and wondrous. Live by the old Scandinavian saying of "there is no such thing as bad weather, only bad clothing". Dance in the rain together! Being outdoors is a great way to build resilience in children especially if the weather is more challenging.

Share in the wonder of the seasons together and the joy of nature as the outdoors really is the most magical place.

75

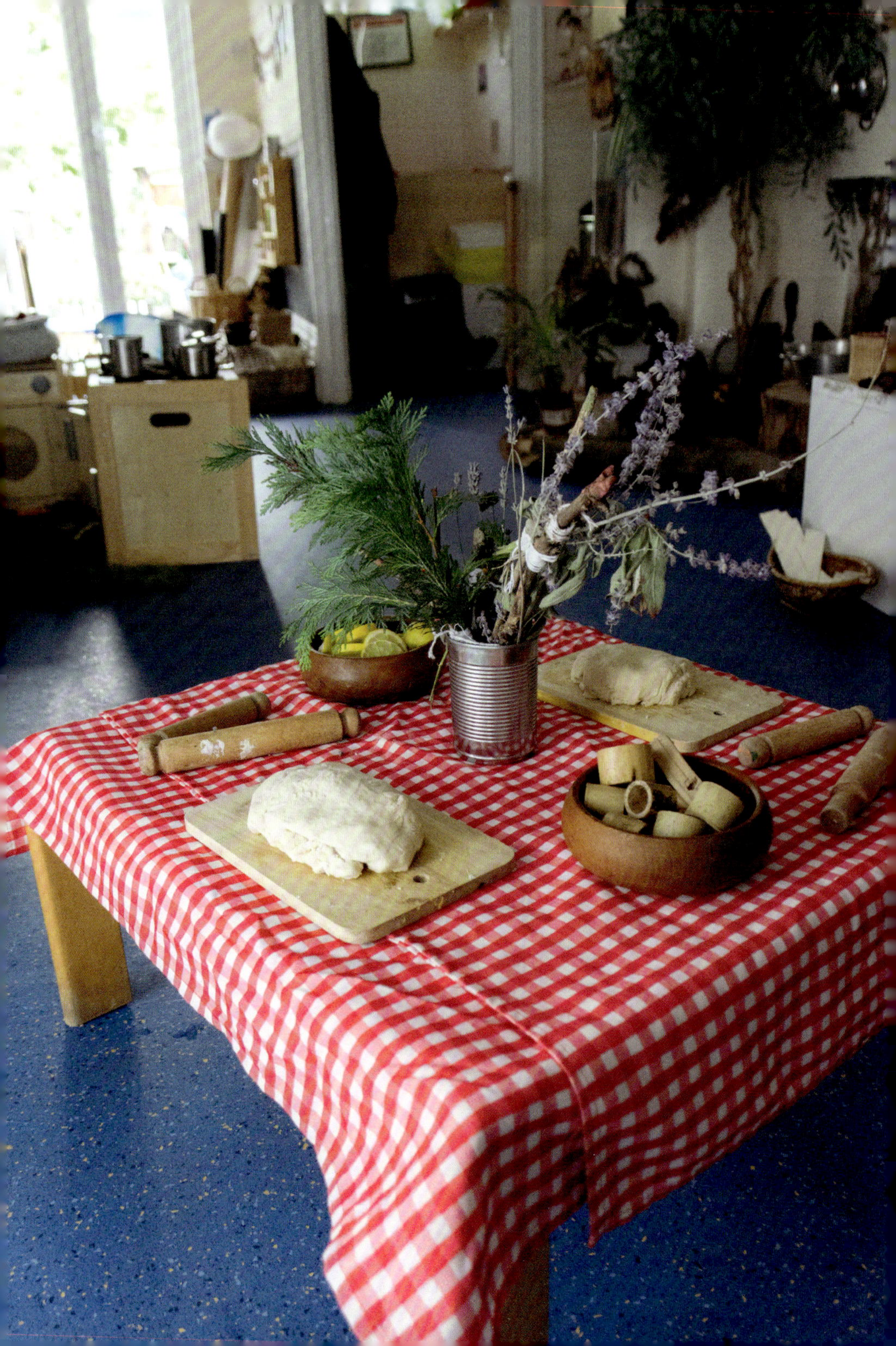

PLAY DOUGH STATION

The play dough station is always a hive of activity with the children engrossed in whatever it is they may be making, thinking and doing. At our Curiosity Approach settings, we feel the play dough station is a valuable place where children come together, to become absorbed in a sensory task, where imagination comes to life. Play dough or any other malleable material can be an experience in which children become completely absorbed, one day they may be fascinated in the creation of scrumptious buns and cakes; another day engrossed in rolling of worms, snakes and snails.

At the same time if several children are being creative at the play dough station then communication and social skills are being developed as they talk about what they are making – it is truly fascinating to be a quiet observer of these activities, but also creates an opportunity to discuss any issues that may arise with their creation, giving an opportunity to problem solve as well.

Our stations offer a wide array of natural resources to add to and extend any creation; glass jars and bottles filled with lentils or pasta. Dried out orange and lemon slices and small cones bring nature to any play dough table or station. Children have the freedom to make play dough from scratch with a visual time table and resources readily at hand. Visual recipe cards and instructions offer children the opportunity to follow the pictures and embark on their own dough creation.

We provide shelving or racking which provides resources close at hand and easily available. Herbs and spices bring a sensory delight, with opportunities for children to cut sprigs of basil, sage, mint or parsley. Lavender is always a firm favourite with children and adults alike, the calming aromatic tones soothe any furrowed brow. Pestles and mortars extend the learning and allow the little learners to crush their selected items and release the aromatic fragrance into the classroom and beyond.

Essential oils and spices, the scent of star of anise captivate a curious mind. Bring velvet tones that touch the nostrils and mind.

Resources are displayed thoughtfully and carefully with some initial order and purpose. Utensils are hung for easy access, allowing children to be the creators of their own learning, mixing ingredients in bowls or powdery, sticky loveliness that transcends into a malleable material we all know as dough.

Chairs are removed, allowing freedom to move around the table, when chairs are introduced, children will only use resources within their arm span. Therefore, it is important we remove the invisible cage a chair creates. Allow children the opportunity to stand, explore freely and without restriction.

Our play dough stations are a useable resource which during the course of any session or day gets messy and disorganized. However thoughtful practitioners are fully aware of the need to reset things again, in preparation for the next day.

Herbs image ID ID 78070536 © Margo555 | Dreamstime

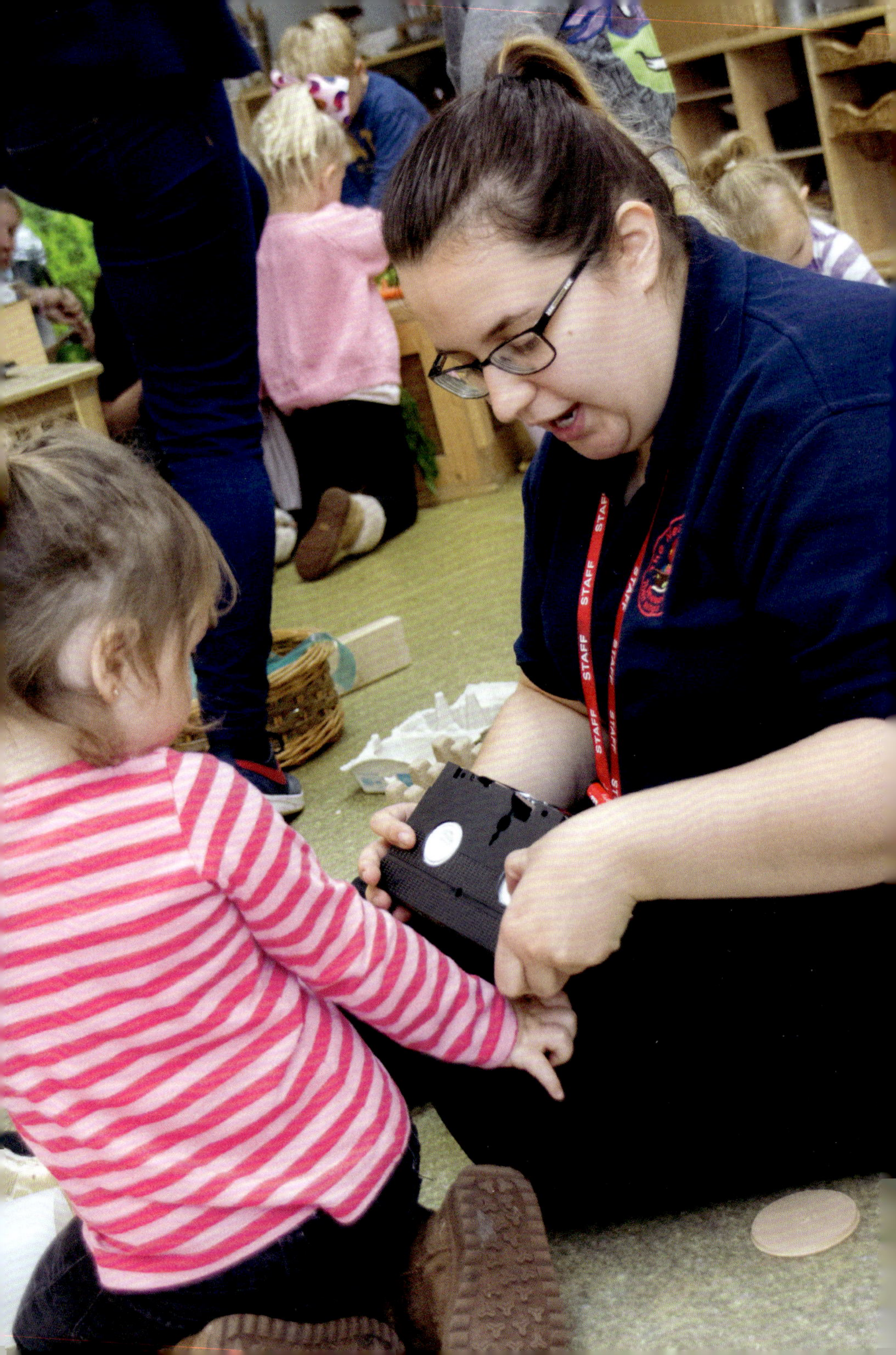
STAFF

QUESTIONS

One of the most important things that we do as early years educators is to engage in conversations with children. We should give careful thought and consideration to our use of questions.

Using open-ended questions can really stretch children's thinking and curiosity, letting us in to the child's mind. Open-ended questions require think time, so be patient as you await a response. If you can answer "yes" or "no" to a question, it is not open-ended, a favourite of ours is "I wonder…".

An open-ended question has no right or wrong answer, so the language involved in formulating an answer can be extensive. As a child puts ideas into words, they will begin to put together innovative and complex ideas and statements. When the educator shows a genuine interest, offers encouragement, clarifies ideas and asks open questions, this supports and extends the children's thinking and helps children to make connections in learning.

In the most effective settings educators support and challenge children's thinking by getting involved in the thinking process with them, through their use of questioning; otherwise known as Sustained Shared Thinking. It is an episode in which two or more individuals 'work together' in an intellectual way to solve a problem, clarify a concept, evaluate activities, extend a narrative etc. Both parties must contribute to thinking and it must develop and extend.

SUSTAINED **= carry on for a reasonable amount of time.**

SHARED **= felt or experienced by more than one.**

THINKING **= it must extend and develop.**

Sustained shared thinking can only happen when there are responsive trusting relationships between adults and children.

When questioning children, be careful not to limit their learning. Let them take it where they are going to take it – this may not be exactly what you had in mind but trust the child to create their own learning path and then challenge them along the way. You'll be pleasantly surprised by the outcome!

ROLE-PLAY

Role-play is an incredibly important part of early childhood. It usually starts on a child's experiences from home. The transformative power of their imagination enables one thing to stand for almost anything else they choose, you see even the one-year old child use representation, the wooden block put by their ear to "speak" to someone on the telephone as they see the adults around them do.

R IS FOR **ROLE-PLAY**

MaKing

Colouring

Cutting

The imagination is an incredibly powerful tool, which as we know is innate in some children but needs gentle encouragement in others. Our early childhood environments should be rich tools for providing children with the opportunity to develop their imagination. In order to accomplish this we must equip the children with spaces, scenarios, props and the support they need to explore their real life or imaginary worlds. Imaginative role-play not only aids intellectual development but also improves children's social skills and their creativity.

R IS FOR **ROLE-PLAY**

> **CHILDREN EXPERIENCE AN ENVIRONMENT WHERE THEIR PLAY IS VALUED AND MEANINGFUL LEARNING AND THE IMPORTANCE OF SPONTANEOUS PLAY IS RECOGNISED.**

Te Whāriki

Have you thought carefully about what is offered to children through role-play within your environment? Responding to their interests and enticing them into a world of imagination. Each child has a home so we should always start by building on from this but do not let this become an adult led space. Think how limiting are your spaces? Is it always a home corner? A vets? A café? Is it over flowing with pretend food? Or do you leave it to the imagination with just some materials, loose parts and authentic resources and let the children construct and create the role-play for themselves? Do you give thought to the presentation or is every space an avalanche of resources that it just becomes one big heap? What does imaginative role–play look like in your setting?

Quote source: Te Whariki published 2017 by the Ministry of Education, New Zealand, copyright © Crown.
Full version available at http://tewhariki.tki.org.nz/en/early-childhood-curriculum-document

S

SENSES

As educators for children, we need to first understand the impact overstimulation has on our little ones, leading to outburst of frustration, fretfulness, tears and tantrums.

Calm neutral colours form the basis for our settings, with the backdrop of magnolia walls and uncluttered spaces. Rooms are set up with thoughtfulness, taking into account the senses of children and adults alike. What does it feel like in your educational setting?

What does it feel like to be at your nursery, what can they see from their own low-level vantage point? Are the displays purposeful? Do they celebrate children's own work or do they document learning? How does it FEEL to be a child within your play space?

Do you have elements of nature within – plants, flowers, nature, water etc?

Do you offer children the opportunity to access authentic resources, loose parts and recycled materials? Resources that allow children opportunities to learn how to think, not what to think.

Are resources thoughtfully presented – inviting children with subliminal messages to come explore, investigate and play?

Does your play space feel homely and inviting and not institutionalized?

Does your play space provide opportunities for quiet time, rest or communication friendly spaces? Space for quieter children to retreat and watch from a secure vantage point? Is it a calm tranquil place or loud and chaotic?

Are resources easily assessible, allowing opportunities for self-selection, promoting independence and opportunities for free choice?

Does your environment offer opportunities for light and shadow, with natural light within each room?

These are just a few questions you need to ask yourself about your own play space.

Have you viewed it down on the floor, from your knees recently? Do you lay on the floor and view the environment with fresh eyes, seeing it through the eyes of the children within?

Get it drastically wrong and you could have unhappy children who may become fretful and unengaged or over-stimulated with feelings of anxiety and stress. Children's mood and behaviour may become affected. Tantrums may occur as they become frustrated and emotional. They are confined to the ever-closing atmosphere with no means of escape!

When you walk into a Curiosity Approach setting, the environment feels calm and tranquil. Soft lavender or lemon grass aromas filter gently across the room. Twinkly fairy lights are thoughtfully positioned to add magic and wonder to play spaces. Battery operated tea lights glow softly around the room.

Gone are the bright primary colours and painted windows, natural light cascades into the room as sunbeams dance playfully across mirrored tables to floor and walls. Rich luxurious tones of polished wooden artifacts and resources add richness to the play space, replacing the plastic toys that all feel and smell the same.

Our senses soak in the tranquility of the space. A wondrous boutique beauty that provides a unhurried basis for learning and development. A feast for the senses that is peaceful, understated and calm.

T IS FOR **TREASURE HUNTERS**

TREASURE HUNTERS

Ahoy there me hearties! 'The Curiosity Approach®' Armada is an eclectic approach to early years, an environment of curiosity, awe and wonder a place for adults to seek out treasure and offer it as an opportunity to explore, discover learn and play.

TREASURE! Beautiful authentic resources rescued from car boots, charity shops and garage sales up and down the land, turning trash into treasure! Bright shiny beautiful items, eclectic random treasure that captures the imagination of both child and educator. Resources that offer value to play, bringing a mix of textures and stimuli that no plastic tea set can offer. Play spaces transform from bright coloured overload to a treasure trove of visual beauty that is individual to the items collected. Who wouldn't want to learn, play and explore in a treasure basket of shiny unusual items? And to feel like you've been transported to a magical place where deep learning comes to life.

Treasure is everywhere, it's the dissuaded items cast aside because they are no longer deemed modern or stylish. It's the tea sets and trays tucked at the back of kitchen cupboards or garage shelves. It's the collection of knick-knacks adorned on grandmas display cabinet. It's the unusual, unique – it's the artifacts collected from far travelled lands. It's the unloved items.

u

UNUSUALLY UNIQUE

The Curiosity Approach® is about inspiring the mind, body and heart! Too often it's easy to forget the educators and practitioners – the adults in our settings!

Remember that you are a family, a team and a unit. Together you achieve more. So, let's start respecting each other, taking time to listen to each other and coming together as individuals. Not just a faceless unit but unique, different people. Sometimes complex, sometimes frustrating but always people who you work with and spend an incredible amount of time with. These unique individuals are your tribe and in every tribe there is always a coming together, an opportunity for shared ideas, shared common ground... a community!

Create an environment of trust and respect. Celebrate your team's achievements and use your meeting time to collaborate ideas and thinking. Celebrate their unique little ways, their quirkiness and differences. Celebrate that each one of your tribe is different and special and contributes to the daily running of the setting. From the manager of your setting to the apprentice or cleaner. From the cook to the administrator – celebrate the contributions they bring to your setting and the skills they have to offer.

Create time to bring your tribe together, a time to collaborate ideas and thinking. To reflect on all the amazing achievements over the past few weeks and months. Change the way you operate your staff meetings, change your mindset and arrange meetings that take account of the unique individuals who make up your team.

Firstly it's important to remember that when educating children, we all recognize that learning happens best when children are active, when they learn by doing not by prescriptive preaching. So why is it we STOP following our own advice when it comes to adults? Why do we expect them to be engaged and interested when we sit them down after a long hard day? Sit them confined to a chair and drone on at them!

Usually staff meetings start with the negative stuff, the moans the groans. The stuff they failed to do! What about all the amazing stuff they did right? The hard work and effort they put in over the last few weeks or months. It can't all have been horrendous?

Think of the positives and focus on those, chat about them. Discuss and celebrate the incredible achievements of the unusually unique.

Like children, adults switch off when there is something they don't want to hear. Shutters go up and they zone out! You've lost their attention and their interest and your team is now on the defensive. It's now you against them. Your team is no longer united – well maybe they are, however it's now you against them. Reflect on this. There is nothing more incredible than seeing your team's eyes light up when food, music, fun and laughter are involved.

Use the time to engage in some collaborative art work for your setting, work together to create a hanging mobile, room signs. Create a belonging tree with inspirational quotes and staff names. Help them see that you are all a family and they have made an important impression on the nursery/setting.

FEED their heart body, mind and soul. Celebrate the unusually unique.

VALUE

The Curiosity Approach® is an eclectic mix of inspirational philosophies and thinking from the recipe book of early years pioneers and global approaches stirred carefully and thoughtfully together with knowledge and understanding from a wealth of experience and amazing ideas. Each piece special in its own unique way, brings value to the wider picture of our modern-day interpretation of The Curiosity Approach®.

If you imagine that each piece of The Curiosity Approach® is a golden thread interwoven into a glorious tapestry of curiosity awe and wonder. Each golden thread carefully and delicately intertwined to make up this incredible picture. Just like New Zealand's philosophy of Early Years education which depicts the woven mat and the artistry of the weaver.

With each of these golden threads, such as environment, senses, tribe, authentic resources and many more, we as adults and thoughtful and mindful practitioners must value the elements of this approach. We must be grateful for the golden threads that create the bigger picture.

Environment

How can you expect children to reach their full potential, if we as adults are not providing them with the environment in which to learn, discover and develop. The environment is the third teacher, treat her well and children will have the opportunity to play and learn in an opportunity rich play space.

People

Value your tribe, for these people are your team, your family. The ones who understand your flaws and love you anyway. The people who inspire and encourage you. Surround yourself with people who see your value and surround you with it.

Resources

Value play, forget giving children imitation items, forget giving children the pretend stuff. Value the children and their play by giving them the real deal. Never underestimate their potential and their ability to be capable confident learners.

Time and space

Value time and space by stepping back and seeing the value in a pause or silence. To carefully step back and observe the incredible learning and development unfolding before your eyes. Unhurried and unrushed to disturb or interrupt the complex array of effective learning that is innate in each and every child. Valuing the child's desire to be independent and work out the solutions untainted by the adults interference or haste to deliver an answer.

Value yourself as an important part in the amazing resource, you are incredible. Your knowledge as a curious passionate early year's educator is incredibly valuable in the child's experience through early years. Without you asking open ended questions and providing unique opportunities for awe and wonder, these children would not be equipped to become the thinkers and doers of the future.

Value your skills, the resources, talents and experiences you bring to the table. Value yourself because there is nobody else in the world like you and you are incredible. Take time to value your passion and excitement for early years. If you have passion, you will never work a day in your life.

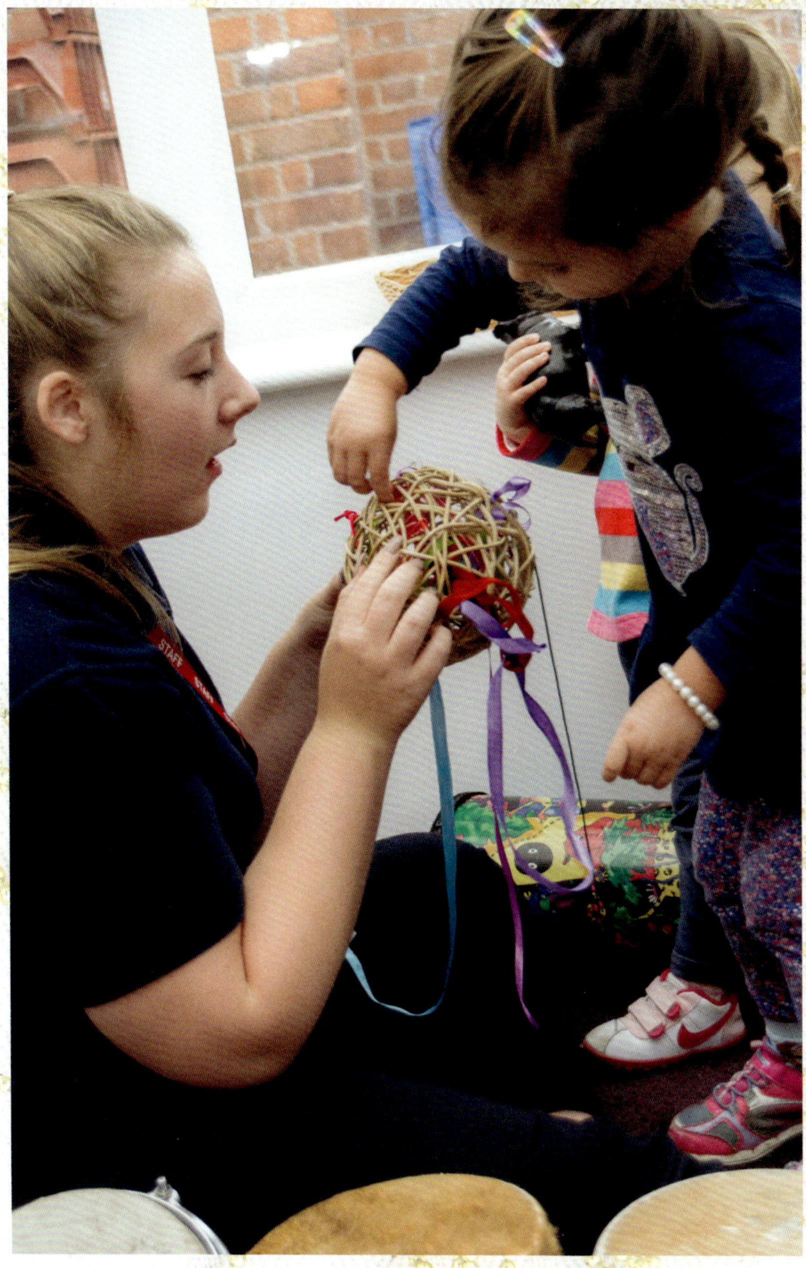
STAFF

W IS FOR **WINTER WONDERLAND**

WINTER WONDERLAND

Creating spaces that inspire curiosity awe and wonder, spaces that capture children's imagination, drawing them in to a place of whimsical magic and imagination. Within one of our Curiosity Approach settings we were lucky enough to have the space to create a magical winter wonderland. A space that was initially created through the interest of the Disney film, Frozen. Over the months the room has evolved, changed and been added to, but ultimately it remains the same.

Large paper lanterns and silver glitter balls hang in careful coordination from the ornate ceiling. Low level mirrored tables and light boxes bring other dimensions to the room. Mirrored lights dance like fairies across the room. This room is a magical wonderland to entice any young child.

An overhead projector cascaded the shadow of delicate lace upon the expanse of clear wall.

Silver vent tubing snakes across the carpet enticing the children to come and play.

The room is a smörgåsbord of loveliness, reflective resources twinkle and shine in the sunlight. Glass nuggets used for matching and sorting. For filling and emptying from one silver dish to another.

Baskets of loose parts are available for self-selection, filled with silver birthday parcel bows, tinsel, clear plastic bottle tops. Silver bangles hung carefully on the branches of a silver mug tree. They delicately ring as they hit the slim silver arms.

Small world arctic animals sit motionless on imaginary icebergs waiting patiently for the young learners to return and continue their game. Fairy lights add a magical touch to this exquisite play space.

104

W IS FOR **WINTER WONDERLAND**
Background Image ID 83460716 © Diianadimitrova | Dreamstime

A selection of loose parts are arranged carefully on the shelving, ready for the opportunity to build and construct. Offering opportunities for problem solving, mathematical concepts of size, shape and measure. Critical thinking is encouraged through the use of these intelligent resources.

This play space is an environment of opportunity, a place to enter and learn following a child's own learning style – to learn HOW to think and not WHAT to think.

105

X

EXTRAORDINARY
...think outside the box!

Traditionally nurseries have all followed the same colourful approach: a universal world of primary colours, cartoon figures and plastic toys have been the norm in many environments.

Through The Curiosity Approach®, it is time to think outside the box and remove the limitations that 'normal' play spaces have encompassed. Start to transform your nursery environment, childminding business or school to reflect your children and team within it...

Ways to create little pockets of wonder and curiosity:

So many wondrous ideas are available, all we need to do as passionate early years educators is to think outside the box and to make the environment extraordinary.

You need to go the extra mile to think beyond the norm, to use your own imagination, to be curious, have fun and make a difference to the experiences you provide and the environments you create.

Try using drain pipes for book shelving.

Twigs and branches create beautiful frames for any artistic creation or photo.

Crates can be used for shelving or a play kitchen. Books adorn every play space or provocation, not just isolated to a singular book corner.

Cots or old cabin beds become large dens for role play or another space to encourage language and conversation.

Picnic baskets turned sideways to create little communication dens, where children can clamber underneath and feel that sense of security and belonging.

Pebble image ID 10978955 © Oleksii Sergieiev | Dreamstime

Each environment follows the children's unique learning style, so each Curiosity Approach setting will be extraordinary in its own special way, because it's reflective of the children and adults within it. It's influenced by the experiences and interests of those who spend time within.

X IS FOR **EXTRAORDINARY… THINK OUT OF THE BOX**

109

It's not about being clones that follow the latest trend. The Curiosity Approach® is about thinking outside the box and ensuring that it meets the individual needs of the children within.

Be curious

Have fun

Make a difference

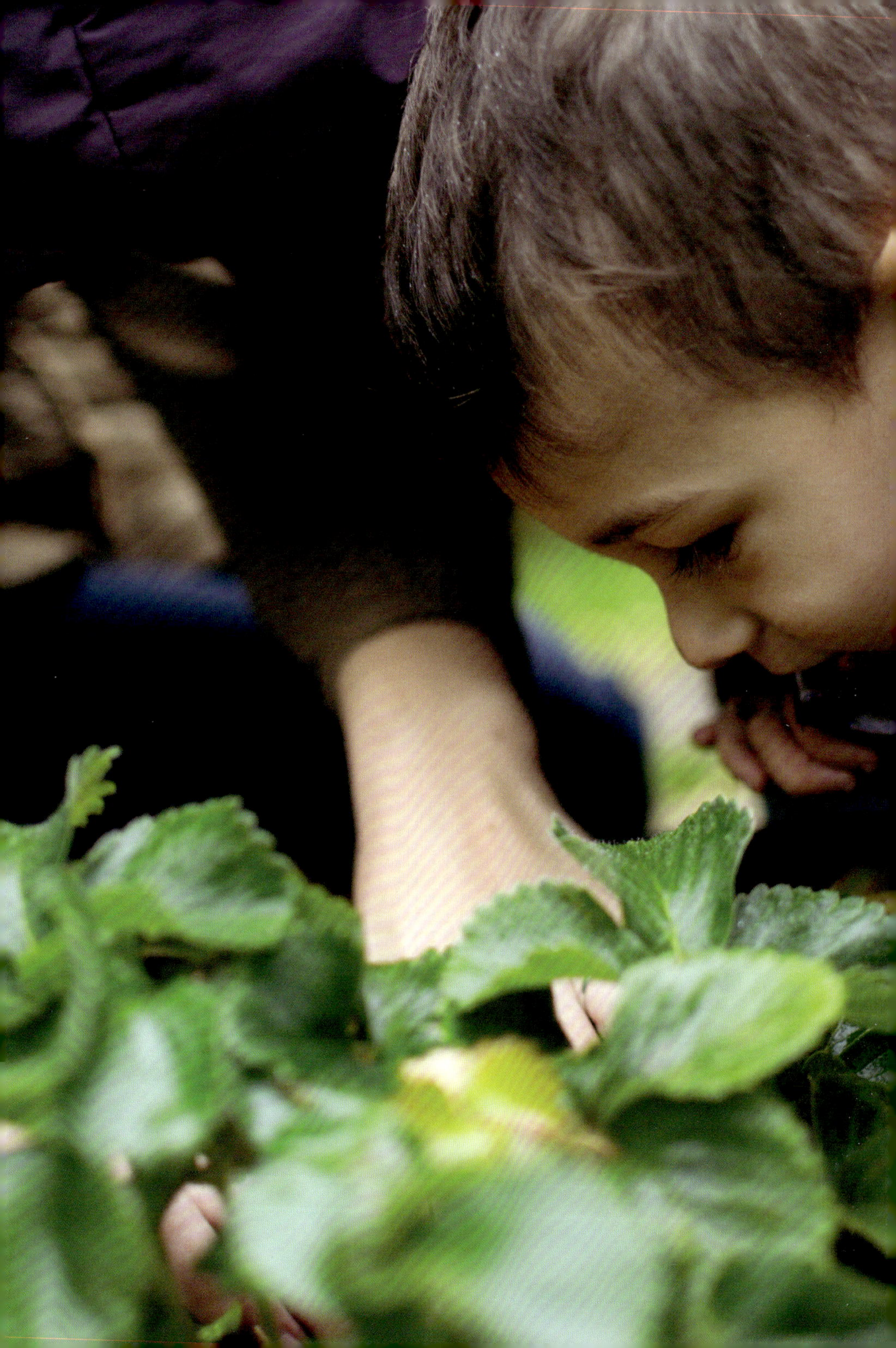

> "PLAY IS THE WAY CHILDREN DISCOVER THEMSELVES - STARTING WITH THEIR FINGERS AND TOES AND GRADUALLY INCLUDING THEIR WHOLE BODY, THEIR EMOTIONS, AND THEIR MINDS."
>
> *Joan Almon*

YOUNG ABSORBENT MINDS

Maria Montessori observed that children regardless of culture, experience the same stages of development at approximately the same ages; children learn to walk, talk, lose teeth all at around the same age. Those other developmental milestones, that are much harder to see, the ones that take place in the child's mind are equally as significant. Montessori called this developmental period the 'Absorbent Mind' stage.

Quote source: p10, Adventure: The value of risk in children's play, published by the Alliance for Childhood, Annapolis, MD (2013).

Children in their earliest years have absorbent minds, they effortlessly soak everything up like a sponge. This is a period of massive brain development for the child, with the most rapid part in the first three years of life. The child's brain grows as she or he sees, feels, tastes, smells and hears. Each time the child uses one of the senses, a connection is made in the child's brain. Experiences repeated help make new connections, which shape the way the child thinks, feels, behaves and learns now and in the future.

The experiences are called play.

Y IS FOR **YOUNG ABSORBENT MINDS**

Professor Karen Hutchison of Rowan University said that children's way of preparing themselves for their roles as adults is play – it is the 'work' of a child. Play is the vehicle to fundamental life long skills; play is the work of childhood. Play is under the control of the child, they decide what, who with and for how long (mostly). Play is imaginative, open-ended and completely amazing!

Through The Curiosity Approach® we strive to provide rich environments that stimulates children's natural curiosity, creativity, awe and wonder. Early childhood environments that are fundamentally based on the necessity of learning through play.

> **CREATIVITY, CURIOSITY, PLAY AND PROBLEM-SOLVING ARE ALL INTERTWINED IN EARLY CHILDHOOD.**
>
> *Joan Almon*

Quote source: It's Playtime. The value of play in early education, and how to get teachers on board (2013).

ZEN

Zen originated in China centuries ago and cannot be explained as a philosophy or in defined terms. It is a number of teachings that need to be experienced, following the learners own journey and understanding. This resonates with the hands-on learning process that children go through and why it fits so perfectly well with The Curiosity Approach®.

As you enter a Curiosity Approach setting, it feels different to a traditional nursery, day care or educare provision. Zen encompasses mindfulness and the feelings of mental wellbeing. Time and space for happiness, health and most importantly love. A non-prescriptive approach to education, where children learn HOW to think and not WHAT to think. A place far removed from any institutionalised schooling or centre.

At Curiousity Approach settings, you see the difference in the interior, you feel the difference in the atmosphere. As the door opens whether into a small foyer or a large entrance hall, the calm and order, a tranquil spa like space that greets every visitor. Gone are the primary colours, the messy and un-loved notice boards with flyers from 12 months previous, the curled up, tatty leaflets and the waft of stale, stagnating nappies that sadly chokes many a nursery establishment.

At The Curiosity Approach®, educational settings feel homely, tranquil and calm. Neutral décor, accompanied with lush green foliage from healthy plants. An array of textures to feast the eyes. Notices, signs and certificates are showcased in well-appointed photo frames – unique ways of displaying the formal documentation all settings need to have on show.

Fairy lights twinkle and shine, entwined around hanging branches or thoughtfully positioned displays and notices. Adding a enchanted magic to any space, enticing children to come inside to an environment that is created with love and passion for early years.

Safely positioned diffusers offer a faint, yet welcoming aroma of lemon grass or lavender to delight the nostrils. Playing gently is the sound of tranquil spa music or calming beat of a far-flung rain forest.

This place already feels magical and wondrous! Nothing about this space feels staid, stilted or stiff. It feels welcoming and peaceful – a place of honesty and trust. A place to tempt the senses, to entice the visitor adult or child to explore more.

THIS IS OUR HAPPY PLACE

Together we can make a difference!

Be part of the change for our children of today, the adults of tomorrow!

The Curiosity Approach® pedagogy recognises learning is "everywhere and anywhere". We understand that from the minute a child enters one of our settings, the children are revered and respected, we give time and energy to every step of the day. We look at the environment as "the third teacher" or as our own "work best friend".

> "WHEN MANY LITTLE PEOPLE IN MANY LITTLE PLACES DO MANY LITTLE THINGS, THEN THE WHOLE WORLD CHANGES."
>
> *Michael Franti*

Would you like your team to have such an attitude?
Would you like your staff to care about their environment?
Would you want them to see that potential is in every corner or every minute of the day?

From transitions to the bathroom, lunchtimes or even the task of putting on a coat, or outdoor clothes. Working in early years education is a mentally stressful job. As educators, we have to be always on high alert! We are continually observing, supervising and ensuring the care and safety of children within our care. Inevitably, some team members need additional encouragement and guidance. They need support and a little helping hand.

The beauty of The Curiosity Approach® is that it combines so many amazing, well researched, proven and documented pedagogies and philosophies.

Would you like your team to see beyond the traditional norms, to stop relying on plastic toys and manufactured items? Would you like your tribe to look through fresh eyes and see the potential of your new and rejuvenated environment?

Learning is everywhere. We can help!

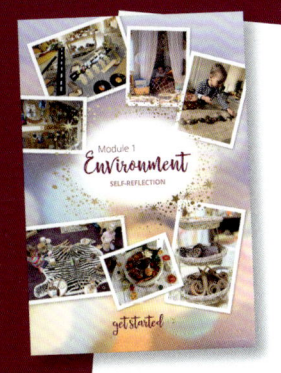

The Curiosity Approach®
ACCREDITATION TOOL KIT

The Curiosity Approach® Tool Kit has been designed to enable educators to review and reflect on their provisions, environments and opportunities for children. We want to support practitioners to work towards improving quality teaching environments and inquisitive moments for children – to help create the 'thinkers, investigators and doers' of the future and give recognition to your wondrous achievements by celebrating quality practice in early childhood.

With The Curiosity Approach® Tool Kit, you can:

- Create beautiful play spaces for children.
- Understand the benefit of open-ended, natural and recycled materials.
- Identify your strengths and have a clear vision for development.
- Celebrate and share achievements and recognise opportunities for curiosity, awe and wonder in early childhood.
- Provide well thought out provocations for children.
- Develop a whole setting approach.
- Belong to a global community of excellence.

Learn more at
www.thecuriosityapproach.com/accreditation

Curiosity Crib

...the home of our subscription site! Available 24/7, Curiosity Crib is a one stop shop of all things Curiosity Approach from 'Invitations to Learning' Recipes to a community Marketplace with new content added every month.

Find out more at
www.thecuriosityapproach.com/curiosity-crib

The Curiosity Approach POCKET-size

Mini training courses providing overviews of some of the essential ingredients of The Curiosity Approach®.

Find out more at
www.thecuriosityapproach.com
or https://the-curiosity-approach-lounge.thinkific.com

A transformational journey of Early Childhood Settings following The Curiosity Approach®.

AVAILABLE AT amazon.co.uk BUY NOW

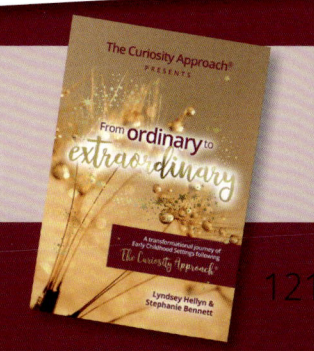

The Curiosity Approach® PRESENTS
From ordinary to extraordinary
A transformational journey of Early Childhood Settings following The Curiosity Approach®
Lyndsey Hellyn & Stephanie Bennett

Be passionate, be inspired... be curious!

Whether you are starting a nursery from scratch or revamping a current early childhood setting, it can be a daunting prospect to ditch the plastic and transform your environment into a natural space – a place that relies heavily on open-ended, recycled materials. This book aims to be a tool, to assist reflection and to move to a new and enlightening way to providing a learning environment for children. Each chapter focusses on a different aspect, from the types of resources to provide, to where to find them, giving you the secret ingredients to setting up subliminal invitations which evoke young children to come and play, engaging in deep levels of engagement and thinking.

We hope this book and its imagery has inspired you. We are eternally grateful to pioneers and philosophies that have paved the way for our approach and to the incredible settings and practitioners across the world, who strive to be extraordinary for the sake of little people. Please help inspire the thinkers and doers of the future, so that they can grow to become equally extraordinary.

123

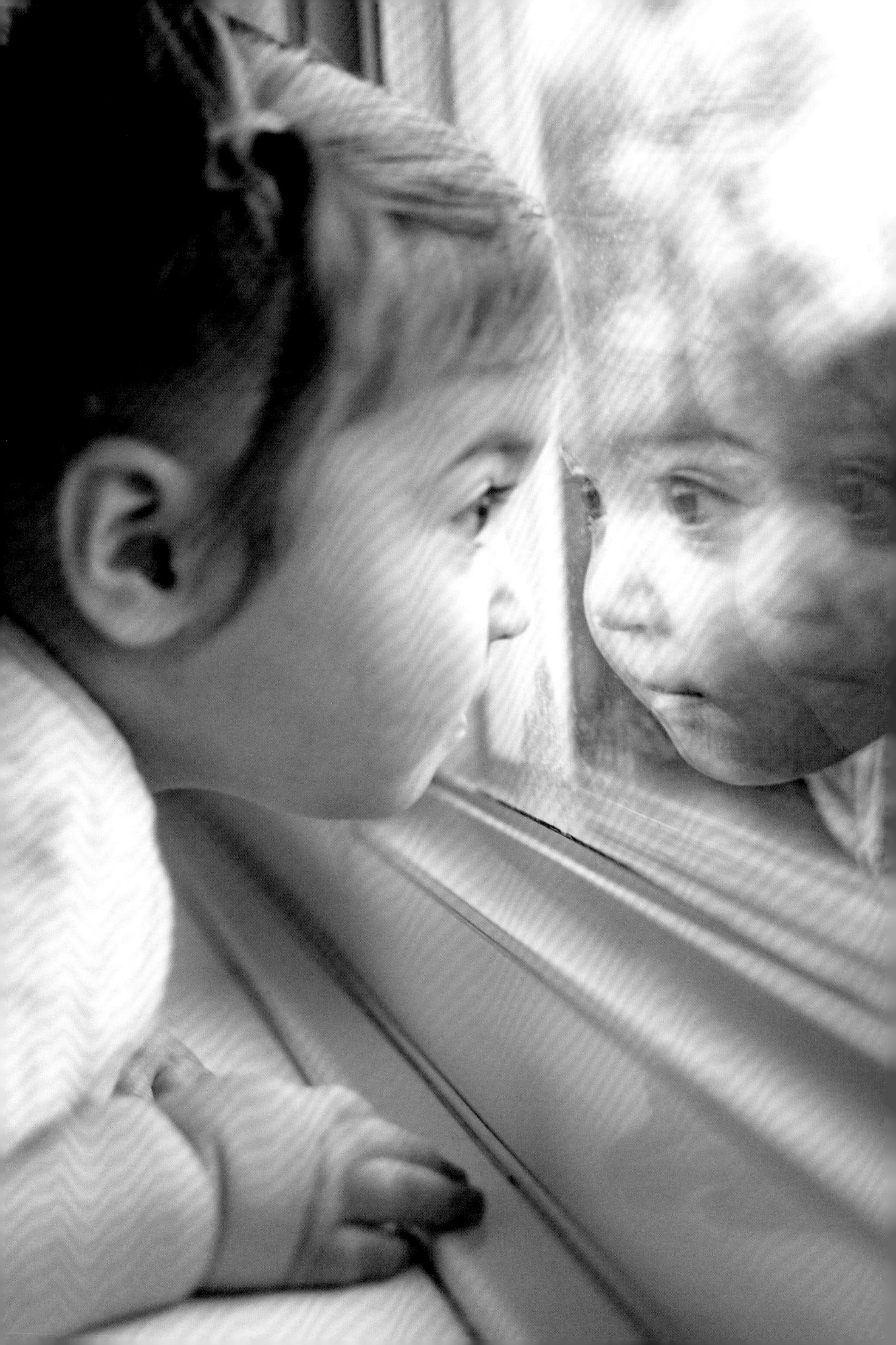